THE GIFT OF
PROPHECY

THE ROLE OF ELLEN WHITE IN GOD'S REMNANT CHURCH

Gerhard Pfandl

Pacific Press® Publishing Association
Nampa, Idaho
Oshawa, Ontario, Canada
www.pacificpress.com

Cover design by Gerald Lee Monks
Cover design resources from Lars Justinen
Inside design by Aaron Troia

Unless otherwise indicated, all italics in quotations are from the original author/source
material.

Unless otherwise indicated, all Scripture quotations are from the New King James Version,
copyright © 1979, 1980, 1982, Thomas Nelson, Inc., Publishers.

Scriptures quoted from RSV are from the Revised Standard Version of the Bible, copyright
© 1946, 1952, 1971 by the Division of Christian Education of the National Council of the
Churches of Christ in the U.S.A. Used by permission.

Scripture quotations marked NIV are from the HOLY BIBLE, NEW INTER-
NATIONAL VERSION . Copyright © 1973, 1978, 1984 by International Bible Society.
Used by permission of Zondervan Publishing House. All rights reserved.

Photo of Arthur G. Daniels (page 113) used by permission of the Department of Archives
and Statistics of the General Conference of Seventh-day Adventists. All other photos courtesy
of the Ellen G. White Estate.

Additional copies of this book are available by calling toll-free 1-800-765-6955 or by visiting
http://www.adventistbookcenter.com.

Library of Congress Cataloging-in-Publication Data

Pfandl, Gerhard.
The gift of prophecy : the role of Ellen White in God's remnant church
/ Gerhard Pfandl.
p. cm.
Includes bibliographical references.
ISBN-13: 978-0-8163-2289-3 (pbk.)
ISBN-10: 0-8163-2289-9 (pbk.)
1. Prophecy—Biblical teaching. 2. White, Ellen Gould Harmon,
1827-1915. I. Title.
BS647.3.P43 2008
231.7'45—dc22
2008026096

08 09 10 11 12 • 5 4 3 2 1

Dedication

To Dr. George Rice, teacher, pastor, and friend

"The greatest work of the *teacher*
is to lead those under his charge
to be intellectual Christians" (1MR 322).

"As the physician deals with physical disease,
so does the *pastor* minister to the sin-sick soul.
And his work is as much more important than that of the physician
as eternal life is more valuable than temporal existence" (GW 338).

"A *friend* loves at all times,
and a brother is born for adversity" (Proverbs 17:17).

Table of Contents

Foreword

Rarely does one encounter a book that is so outstanding that on the last page the reader thinks, *I want to read this again—now!* Yet that is exactly what happened to me when I finished reading Dr. Pfandl's manuscript for this book. Every chapter gripped my heart and mind and increased my appreciation for our wonderful God who communicates His love and counsel through His chosen prophets.

Thus far in my tenure at the Ellen G. White Estate, I have had opportunities to preach in forty-seven countries and five continents concerning Ellen White's prophetic ministry and her relationship to the Scriptures. At virtually every venue, I host a question-and-answer dialogue with the audience, and I've found that many of the questions surface repeatedly regardless of the culture. I am gratified that in *The Gift of Prophecy*, Dr. Pfandl gives succinct, unambiguous, compelling answers to the very questions I have heard from God's remnant people around the world.

Just to whet your appetite about the good things to come, I'll note that teacher, scholar, and pastor Pfandl deals with such questions as How necessary is the human herald in the process of salvation? Is speaking in tongues a genuine gift of the Spirit? In what way does God communicate His messages to prophets? And what is the relationship between the gift of prophecy and God's remnant church?

Dr. Pfandl also treats questions relating specifically to Ellen G. White's ministry, such as Did she believe no person could come to Christ after 1844 (the "shut door" theory)? What is the nature of her authority? Does the Bible corroborate her statement that our sins are forgiven only if we remain faithful? Did every prediction Ellen White made come to pass? Was she a theologian? Was she plagiarizing when she used other authors? On what biblical basis can we have confidence in her writings? Is it possible to misinterpret her writings?

I found Dr. Pfandl's explanations about inspiration as clear and understandable as anything I have encountered in my quite extensive reading about the prophetic gift and particularly about Ellen White's ministry. Though his answers are necessarily condensed for the purposes of this book and thus in some cases may best serve as springboards for the reader's further investigation, I found every page highly beneficial.

Dr. Pfandl is truly a gifted "teacher in Israel." May every reader of *The Gift of Prophecy* be personally strengthened in his or her understanding of God's chain of communication to humanity and become an agent to pass on that understanding to others.

Cindy Tutsch, DMin
Associate Director, Ellen G. White Estate
Silver Spring, Maryland, U.S.A.

Preface

Apart from revelation in nature, God revealed Himself to the church through the Scriptures and the gifts of the Spirit. These methods of communication are part of the divine plan of redemption. The Scriptures do not take the place of the gifts of the Spirit; neither do the gifts of the Spirit take the place of the Scriptures. Both are necessary for the growth and well-being of the church. All who accept the authority of the Bible must also accept the ministry of the Holy Spirit through spiritual gifts, because the teaching concerning these gifts is an integral part of Scripture.

Because of texts such as Ephesians 4:11 and Joel 2:28, 29, Seventh-day Adventists believe that the gifts of the Spirit will be manifested in the church until the Second Coming. This does not mean that all the gifts will be in operation all the time, but whenever God sees the necessity for it, He can, in His sovereignty, bestow any or all the gifts of the Spirit on His people.

In the book of Revelation, God promised that there would be a special manifestation of the prophetic gift in the time of the end (Revelation 12:17; 19:10; 22:8, 9). From the very beginning, Seventh-day Adventists have believed that the gift of prophecy has been manifested in their midst in the life and work of Mrs. Ellen G. White (1827–1915). For seven decades she gave messages of counsel and warning that Seventh-day Adventists believe were just as much from God as were the messages of the biblical prophets.

It is true that Mrs. White's life came to a close in 1915, but her work lives on—her books full of spiritual insights and counsel are still with us. Near the

Preface

close of her life she declared, "Whether or not my life is spared, my writings will constantly speak, and their work will go forward as long as time shall last" (3 SM 76).

At a time when the gift of prophecy is under attack from various quarters, it is the purpose of this book to provide some answers to these attacks. I also want to share with the reader some of the wonderful blessings that have come to God's people throughout the ages through the gift of prophecy. But I particularly want to highlight the blessings that God has bestowed on His remnant people, the Seventh-day Adventist Church, through the prophetic ministry of Ellen G. White.

At this point, I would like to thank the staff of the Ellen G. White Estate at the General Conference for their unfailing support while I was writing this book. May it contribute to the strengthening of Seventh-day Adventists' commitment to and support of the gift of prophecy in God's remnant church.

Abbreviations

BC   *The Seventh-day Adventist Bible Commentary*
      (7 volumes)
GCB   *General Conference Bulletin*
Gr.   Greek
RH   *Review and Herald*
ST   *Signs of the Times*

Ellen G. White books

AA	*The Acts of the Apostles*	MM	*Medical Ministry*
CD	*Counsels on Diet and Foods*	MR	*Manuscript Releases* (21 volumes)
CM	*Colporteur Ministry*	PK	*Prophets and Kings*
COL	*Christ's Object Lessons*	PP	*Patriarchs and Prophets*
CW	*Counsels to Writers and Editors*	RC	*Reflecting Christ*
DA	*The Desire of Ages*	SC	*Steps to Christ*
Ed	*Education*	SG	*Spiritual Gifts* (4 volumes)
Ev	*Evangelism*	SM	*Selected Messages* (3 volumes)
EW	*Early Writings*	SpM	Spaulding–Magan collection
FE	*Fundamentals of Christian Education*	SR	*The Story of Redemption*
FLB	*The Faith I Live By*	T	*Testimonies for the Church* (9 volumes)
GC	*The Great Controversy*	TM	*Testimonies to Ministers and Gospel Workers*
GW	*Gospel Workers*	YRP	*Ye Shall Recieve Power*
HP	*In Heavenly Places*		
LS	*Life Sketches of Ellen G. White*		
LDE	*Last Day Events*		
Mar	*Maranatha*		
MH	*The Ministry of Healing*		

CHAPTER 1

Heaven's Means of Communication

That God has revealed Himself to humanity is foundational to the Christian faith. If God hadn't taken the initiative in making Himself known to us, we would have remained in hopeless darkness. The essence and fullness of God's being is beyond the capacity of human understanding. As Zophar said to Job, " 'Can you search out the deep things of God? / Can you find out the limits of the Almighty?' " In response to his own question, he continued, " 'They are higher than heaven—what can you do? / Deeper than Sheol—what can you know? / Their measure is longer than the earth / And broader than the sea' " (Job 11:7-9). Yet God has so manifested Himself to us that we can know something of Him—indeed, we not only can, but we must to be saved.

The two basic ways in which God has revealed Himself are called *general revelation* and *special revelation*. General revelation is God's revelation of Himself to all people at all times and in all places through nature and people's consciences. Special revelation comprises God's revelations through the prophets as recorded in Scripture and His revelation through Jesus Christ.

General revelation

General revelation is sometimes also called natural revelation in contrast to the supernatural revelation of God recorded in Scripture. The mental, moral, and spiritual qualities of humankind are a manifestation of this general revelation. Human beings were created in the image of God, and in spite of the Fall, we still reflect to a certain degree the character of God. In particular, every human being has moral consciousness. "The main task of conscience is to encourage us to do the right and to avoid the wrong. It also pronounces judgment. This faculty is a universal phenomenon, even though its operation differs from person to person."[1] The concept of the voice of conscience is particularly important to understanding God's justice and the salvation of the heathen.

God's disclosure of Himself through what He has created also constitutes general revelation. It was this that prompted David to exclaim, "The heavens declare the glory of God; / And the firmament shows His handiwork" (Psalm 19:1). In Romans 1:20, Paul argued that all humanity has a rudimentary knowledge of God: "Since the creation of the world His invisible attributes are clearly seen, being understood by the things that are made, even His eternal power and Godhead, so that they are without excuse."

Unfortunately, human beings often miss the message of God in nature. Some become so familiar with God's creation that they take it for granted and don't think about its wonders. Others elevate nature to the position of God and ascribe everything to the laws of nature. Still others turn away from the true knowledge of God and worship the creatures God made or human-made idols and practices. Paul, therefore, wrote in Romans 1 that "God also gave them up to uncleanness . . . God gave them up to vile passions . . . God gave them over to a debased mind" (verses 24, 26, 28).

While nature provides an abundance of examples of God's wonderful creative acts, it also displays the consequences of the Fall. Thorns and thistles, the lion that kills the gazelle to feed its cubs, and the spider that traps the fly all bear evidence to the fact that sin has changed what God at one time pronounced "very good" (see Genesis 1:31). This is also why Ellen White wrote, "Nature still speaks of her Creator. Yet these revelations are partial and imperfect. And in our fallen state, with weakened powers and restricted vision, we are incapable of interpreting aright. We need the fuller revelation of Himself that God has given in His written word" (Ed 16).

Special revelation

Special revelation is generally understood to refer to the revelation recorded in Scripture. Special revelation is "given." It is not something that human beings, left to themselves, can recognize. While general revelation is accessible to all people, special revelation is accessible only to those to whom the Word of God comes either supernaturally or through human agents.

God appeared to Noah, Abraham, Moses, and the Old Testament prophets to make His will known to them. He revealed His power and purpose in the crucial events in Israel's history, and in the fullness of time He sent His Son, who manifested the Father in the garb of humanity. These special revelations have been made Scripture in the sixty-six books of the Old and New Testaments. "The Bible," said Ellen G. White, "is God's voice speaking to us just as surely as though we could hear Him with our ears" (HP 134).

In revealing Himself to His people here on earth, God used a variety of means. The most important are the following:

1. *Theophanies* (appearances of the Deity). The early books of the Bible record many instances of theophany. God appeared directly or in the guise of the Angel of the Lord (see Genesis 17:1, 22; 18:1; 26:2; 32:30; Exodus 3:2-6; 33:11; etc.). The Angel of the Lord—identified as God—was a temporary manifestation of Jesus Christ Himself. According to Scripture, no one but the only begotten Son can make God known (see John 1:18). Thus, in Exodus 23:21, Yahweh said of the Angel of the Lord, " 'My name is in him.' " This Angel was the same One who spoke with Moses on Sinai (see Acts 7:38) and who saved Israel from all her distresses (see Isaiah 63:9).

2. *Visions and dreams.* Scripture specifically mentions visions and dreams as the marks of a true prophet (see Numbers 12:6). Amos introduced his prophecies by saying, "The words of Amos, . . . which he saw concerning Israel" (1:1). In ancient Israel, prophets were also called *seers* (see 1 Samuel 9:9), and the distinguishing mark of false or foolish prophets was precisely this: they " 'have seen nothing!' " (Ezekiel 13:3). Throughout the Old and New Testaments we meet people who received visions and dreams from God (see Genesis 28:12-16; 1 Kings 3:5-15; Daniel 2:19, 28; 7:1; 10:7, 8; Matthew 1:20; Acts 10:9-16; etc.).

The prophets were obviously under the control of the Spirit of God; it is solely by His enabling that anyone can prophesy (see Numbers 11:25, 29; 1 Samuel 10:6, 10). Ezekiel declared that the hand of the Lord was "strong" upon him, that the Spirit lifted him up and took him away, and that He entered into him and set him upon his feet (see Ezekiel 3:14, 22, 24). Micah said that he was filled with power by the Spirit of the Lord to deliver his message (3:8). And in the New Testament, Peter affirmed that the prophets spoke from God, being moved by the Holy Spirit (2 Peter 1:21).

3. *Jesus Christ.* The most important and most complete revelation of God is the incarnation of Jesus Christ. In Him, said Paul, "dwells all the fullness of the Godhead bodily" (Colossians 2:9). Jesus came into the world to reveal the Father's character, His attributes, and, most importantly, the plan of salvation with Himself as the central Figure. Hebrews 1:1, 2 contrasts the earlier revelations of God through the prophets with the appearance of Christ and indicates that the Incarnation was the superior revelation. The revelation of God's character culminated in the life, death, and resurrection of Christ. His words surpassed those of the prophets and apostles. When the prophets spoke, they passed on the messages they received from God; when Jesus spoke, it was God Himself who was speaking. Therefore, He could say, " 'I and My Father are one' " (John 10:30) and " 'He who has seen Me has seen the Father' " (14:9). Ellen White wrote, "God saw that a clearer revelation than nature was needed to portray both His personality and His character. He sent His Son into the world to reveal, so far as could be endured by human sight, the nature and the attributes of the invisible God" (8T 265). In Jesus, God was living among humankind and displaying His attributes to them.

In order to capture for posterity the different facets of Christ's life, the Holy Spirit inspired four Gospels detailing from different angles the all-important three and a half years of Christ's life. The written Word is, of course, subordinate to the Person who is revealed in its pages, but it is the medium that takes us as close to the life of Christ as we can get.

The purpose of God's revelation

The primary purpose of God's revelation to humankind is to acquaint them with the plan of salvation. While here on earth, Jesus preached and taught the plan of salvation to all who were willing to listen. After His ascension, the disciples, empowered by the Holy Spirit, carried on the work that He had begun. Within a few decades, the preaching of the gospel had reached tens of thousands of people throughout the Roman Empire, and less than three hundred years later, Christianity became the dominant religion of the then known world.

But what about the millions and billions of people who have never had the opportunity to hear the gospel of God's love for them? Will they all be lost?

That knowledge of the gospel is necessary for salvation is the general teaching of Scripture. Jesus declared that no one can come to the Father but by Him (see John 14:6). He also stated repeatedly that " 'he who does not believe will be condemned' " (Mark 16:16; cf. John 3:18), and without some knowledge, faith is impossible. In Romans 10, Paul first states that whoever calls on the name of the Lord shall be saved (verse 13), and then he argues, "How then shall they call on Him in whom they have not believed? And how shall they believe in Him of whom they have not heard? And how shall they hear without a preacher? And how shall they preach unless they are sent? . . . So then faith comes by hearing, and hearing by the word of God" (verses 14, 15, 17).

John Stott observed that "the essence of Paul's argument is seen if we put his six verbs in the opposite order: Christ sends heralds; heralds preach; people hear; hearers believe; believers call; and those who call are saved."[2] The opposite, of course, is also true: if no one is sent to preach, people cannot hear, they cannot believe, hence they cannot call, and therefore they are lost.

The apostle John wrote, "He who has the Son has life; he who does not have the Son of God does not have life" (1 John 5:12), and Paul said that to be without Christ is to be without hope (see Ephesians 2:12). According to Peter, salvation is possible only through Jesus Christ (see Acts 4:12). So, the general teaching of Scripture seems to be that unless people hear the gospel of Jesus Christ, they are lost. But what about Romans 2? Does it show another possibility?

The context of Romans 2

In the first three chapters of his letter to the Romans, Paul establishes the theological truths that all human beings are sinners (3:23), and that therefore all deserve the wrath of God, and that all are saved in the same way—"through the redemption that is in Christ Jesus" (3:24).

Paul begins his argument in the latter part of chapter 1, where he repeatedly states that because the Gentiles have refused to acknowledge God, He has "given them up" to their own lusts and passions (see 1:24, 26, 28). They are sinners and therefore "worthy of death" (1:32). Next he turns to the Jews. They would agree with him regarding what he said about the Gentiles, but he tells them, "you are inexcusable" for "in whatever you judge another you condemn yourself; for you who judge practice the same things" (2:1). They are no better than the Gentiles when it comes to obeying God—although they have a greater understanding of God's standard than the Gentiles, they still do evil. Paul sums up his argument in chapter 3: "All [Gentiles and Jews] have sinned and fall short of the glory of God" (3:23).

The issue in Romans 2:11-16 is the accountability—not the salvation—of Jews and Gentiles. The fact that God is no respecter of persons (verse 11) is illustrated by what Paul says in verse 12. "As many as have sinned without law will also perish without law, and as many as have sinned in the law will be judged by the law." Those "without law" are the Gentiles, who do not have the written law that God gave the Israelites on Mount Sinai. However, the Gentiles won't perish because they didn't have the written law. They will perish because they are sinners.

On what basis can they be said to be sinners? They are sinners because they have transgressed against the law "written in their hearts, their conscience" (2:15). What is written in their hearts is not the new covenant mentioned in Jeremiah 31:31-34 but the deeds or conduct required by the law. Jack Blanco's expanded paraphrase of Romans 2:15 says, "They give evidence that the principles of the law are written in their hearts because their consciences are guided by God."[3] Among the Gentiles, conscience performed the same function as the law performed among the Jews.

This passage, therefore, cannot be used to argue that the Gentiles who have never heard the gospel will be saved on the basis of their obedience to their conscience, because this would be salvation by works. Furthermore, we must remember that this passage is not speaking about salvation but about judgment (2:16). Paul contrasts two groups of people, the privileged Jews, who have the written law of God, and the less privileged Gentiles, who do not. How can God be fair to both and judge them impartially? Each, says Paul, will be judged by the method appropriate to their case. The Jews will be judged by the written law and the Gentiles by the unwritten law of their conscience. Judged in this way, both groups will be found to be sinners. The Jews, it will be found, have sinned against the written law of God, and the Gentiles have sinned against the unwritten law of their conscience. The outcome, therefore, is the same for both groups—they are all sinners, and they are all lost. Each can be saved only through the substitutionary death of Jesus on the cross.

The statement that the Gentiles "do by nature the things in the law" refers to the fact that even pagans practice things stipulated by the law of God, "such as the pursuit of lawful vocations, the procreation of offspring, filial and natural affection, the care of the poor and sick, and numerous other natural virtues which are required by the law."[4] In that sense they "are a law to themselves" (2:14)—in other words, they have a general knowledge of God's requirements for a virtuous life. Nevertheless, it is important to remember that even if a Gentile lived up to all the law that his conscience reveals to him, this could not save him because that would be salvation by works, something Paul clearly denies. Throughout his writings Paul hammers home the truth that "a man is justified by faith apart from the deeds of the law" (Romans 3:28; see also Galatians 2:16; Ephesians 2:8, 9; etc.).

One of the purposes of the written law, as well as of the law of conscience, is to provide a basis for God's judgment. While the Gentiles have no explicit knowledge of the written law, God can still judge them "in the day when God will judge the secrets of men" (Romans 2:16) because they have transgressed against their conscience-law. On Judgment Day no one will have an excuse; no one will be able to say, "Lord, how can You judge me? I didn't know anything about Your law." That day will reveal that all, Jews and Gentiles alike, have sinned, because " 'There is none righteous, no, not one' " (Romans 3:10).

Thus, Romans 2 is in harmony with the general teaching of the rest of Scripture. There is only one way of salvation—Jesus Christ (see John 14:6). " 'This is eternal life, that they may know You, the only true God, and Jesus Christ whom You have sent' " (John 17:3). Paul therefore says, "I count everything as loss because of the surpassing worth of knowing Christ Jesus my Lord" (Philippians 3:8, RSV).

Jesus' commission, " 'Go therefore and make disciples of all the nations' " (Matthew 28:19), and the knowledge that there is only one way of salvation (see Acts 4:12) have comprised the driving force behind Christian mission. The conviction that people will be lost unless they hear the gospel has sent thousands of missionaries into lands where the name of Christ was unknown.

Does this mean that everyone who doesn't hear the gospel is therefore automatically lost?

Ellen White and the salvation of the heathen

Throughout her writings, Ellen White urged the church to fulfill its God-given responsibility to bring the gospel to those who don't know Christ. She clearly understood that many people will be lost because the gospel wasn't brought to them. "The world is in need of the saving truth that God has entrusted to His people. The world will perish unless it be given a knowledge of God through His chosen agencies" (TM 459), and "Multitudes perish for want of Christian teaching. Beside our own doors and in foreign lands the heathen are untaught and unsaved" (MH 288). In the book *Education* she wrote, "Millions upon millions have never so much as heard of God or of His love revealed in Christ. It is their right to receive this knowledge. They have an equal claim with us in the Saviour's mercy. And it rests with us who have received the knowledge, with our children to whom we may impart it, to answer their cry" (Ed 263).

Ellen G. White (1827–1915)

Though Ellen White spoke of millions upon millions of people going into Christless graves because the gospel is not brought to them, she also taught that there are occasions when God, apart from human messengers, reaches out to individuals in heathen lands and brings the gospel to them:

Those whom Christ commends in the judgment may have known little of theology, but they have cherished His principles. Through the influence of the divine Spirit they have been a blessing to those about them. Even among the heathen are those who . . . worship God ignorantly, those to whom the light is never brought by human instrumentality, yet they will not perish. Though ignorant of the written law of God, they have heard His voice speaking to them in nature, and have done the things that the law required. Their works are evidence that the Holy Spirit has touched their hearts, and they are recognized as the children of God (DA 638).

Heaven's plan of salvation is broad enough to embrace the whole world. God longs to breathe into prostrate humanity the breath of life. And He will not permit any soul to be disappointed who is sincere in his longing for something higher and nobler than anything the world can offer. Constantly He is sending His angels to those who, while surrounded by circumstances the most discouraging, pray in faith for some power higher than themselves to take possession of them and bring deliverance and peace. In various ways God will reveal Himself to them and will place them in touch with providences that will establish their confidence in the One who has given Himself a ransom for all, "that they might set their hope in God, and not forget the works of God, but keep His commandments." Psalm 78:7 (PK 377, 378).

In each of these cases, the Holy Spirit or the angels of God are reaching out to these individuals and implanting the grace of God in their hearts. These heathen are not saved because they have done the works their conscience told them to do. As we have said, this would be salvation by works. They are saved because the Holy Spirit has touched their hearts and revealed God's love to them. However, such cases are the exceptions and not the rule.

Ellen White's comments regarding the salvation of the heathen fall into three categories: (1) The majority of her statements make it clear that God's general way of saving the heathen is through the church.[5] (2) Some quotations indicate that God brings honest people among the heathen in contact with the gospel.* (3) And in some cases, God, through the Holy Spirit, speaks to individuals in heathen lands and brings them the gospel without any human messengers.[†] Such occasions, however, are not the rule but the exception.

God's justice

Some will object to this teaching and argue that God's justice requires that every person receive an opportunity for salvation. While this seems perfectly logical, it is nevertheless unscriptural. Ezekiel 3:18 and 33:8 teach that the watchman is to warn the wicked so he can mend his ways. If he is not

---

* In Scripture we have Rahab and Cornelius. Modern examples would be the Davis Indians in Guyana and Sekuba, the bushman, in the Kalahari Desert.
† Only heaven will reveal how many there have been over the millennia.

warned, God says, he will die in his sins, but the watchman is held responsible. Similarly, Romans 10 teaches that it is the responsibility of those who know the gospel to pass it on, and if this is not done, people will be lost.

It is sad but not unjust that sinners will perish. If they are lost, they are lost because they are sinners, not because they have not had the opportunity to be saved.

What will happen to those who have never had an opportunity to hear the gospel? Abraham said, " 'Shall not the Judge of all the earth do right?' " (Genesis 18:25). That Judge certainly will. Of some of the slaves in colonial America, Ellen White wrote,

> I saw that the slave master will have to answer for the soul of his slave whom he has kept in ignorance; and the sins of the slave will be visited upon the master. God cannot take to heaven the slave who has been kept in ignorance and degradation, knowing nothing of God or the Bible, fearing nothing but his master's lash, and holding a lower position than the brutes. But He does the best thing for him that a compassionate God can do. He permits him to be as if he had not been, while the master must endure the seven last plagues and then come up in the second resurrection and suffer the second, most awful death. Then the justice of God will be satisfied (EW 276).

What happens to those slaves may well happen to "millions of human beings . . . bound down under false religions, in the bondage of slavish fear, of stolid indifference, toiling like beasts of burden, bereft of hope or joy or aspiration here, and with only a dull fear of the hereafter" (DA 478), who have never had an opportunity to accept salvation.

So, Scripture and the Spirit of Prophecy teach that there is only one name under heaven whereby we can be saved (see Acts 4:12). While in general God saves the heathen through the preaching of the gospel, sometimes bringing them in contact with missionaries, there are occasions when He intervenes directly—through the Holy Spirit touching the hearts of people to bring salvation to them without any human agent. Why He does so in some cases and not in others only He knows. However, knowing that billions of people have never even heard the name of Jesus should motivate every Christian to do all he or she can to spread the good news worldwide.

CHAPTER 2

The Prophetic Gift

Prophets and prophecies were known in the ancient Near East outside of the Bible. The Mari texts from Mesopotamia (eighteenth century B.C.) refer to "prophets" (*nabu*) who provided guidance for the kings through their omens. In ancient Egypt, a special class of priests called "servants of god" interpreted dreams and oracles (cf. Genesis 41). The Egyptian story of Wen-Amun records that while Wen-Amun was in Phoenicia (ca. 1090 B.C.), a young attendant at the Phoenician court fell into a trance and delivered an oracle authenticating Wen-Amun's mission.[1]

Throughout history, individuals have made predictions, some of which came to pass. In the sixteenth century, Nostradamus supposedly "foresaw and predicted almost every major historical event in France and crises in many other countries."[2] Tycho Brahe, the official astrologer to Rudoph II of Austria, is said to have predicted, two years before it happened, the Great Plague that swept Europe in 1665. In April 1929, based on the dream of a broker who had consulted him, the psychic Edgar Cayce predicted a stock market crash. Six months later the great Wall Street crash occurred. And in the summer of 1961, Jean Dixon reportedly foretold that Dag Hammer-skjöld, the UN secretary general, would be killed in a plane crash in mid-September. Hammerskjöld lost his life in a plane crash on September 18, 1961.[3] Were all these people inspired by God? Did they have the biblical gift of prophecy?

In Scripture, the individuals whom God endowed with the gift of prophecy were people who walked with God. They weren't sinless, but they did strive to live in harmony with God's revealed will. They had a personal relationship with God. There is no evidence that this was the case with the psychics mentioned above. How then could they make such accurate predictions?

Speaking of the idols at Ekron (see 2 Kings 1:2), Ellen White wrote, "The predictions there uttered, and the information given, proceeded directly from the prince of darkness. It is Satan who created, and who maintains the worship of idols, to divert the minds of men from God. It is by his agency that the kingdom of darkness and falsehood is supported" (RH, June 27, 1882). Satan is well able to predict events and then make them happen.

The patriarchs as prophets

The Hebrew word *nabi* (prophet) refers to a person whom God has called to communicate His messages to humankind. *Nabi* is related to the ancient Babylonian verb *nabu,* "to call." In Babylon the king was repeatedly addressed as "the one called (*nibît*) by the great gods."[4] Thus, a prophet was someone who had received a divine call and who was generally an independent religious and charismatic figure. "He had no hereditary claim to the office, nor could he appropriate the title of *nābhî'* by virtue of political appointment."[5]

We don't usually think of Noah as a prophet, but Scripture says he walked with God (see Genesis 6:9) and received messages from Him (see 6:13, 14; 7:1; 8:15). Noah was about 480 years old when God announced that He was going to destroy the earth with a flood (see 6:3; cf. 7:6). Heeding God's instructions, Noah built a ship in which he and his family were saved (see 7:7, 13; 1 Peter 3:20). However, Noah did more than simply build an ark to save his family, for 2 Peter 2:5 says that he was "a preacher of righteousness." For 120 years he warned his fellow citizens of the impending catastrophe, but only a few believed and were saved (see 1 Peter 3:20).

Not much is known about the prophet Enoch. He also walked with God, Scripture says, and he was translated to heaven without dying (see Genesis 5:24). In Hebrews 11 he is listed among the heroes of faith, and Jude mentions the tradition that Enoch proclaimed the Second Coming and God's judgment on the ungodly (see Jude 14, 15).

The Prophetic Gift

The first person called a prophet in the Bible is Abraham (see Genesis 20:7). After he told Abimelech, king of Gerar, that Sarah was his sister, and after Abimelech had sent for her, God spoke to Abimelech in a dream and threatened to destroy him if he came near Sarah. When Abimelech protested that he had acted with " 'a clear conscience and clean hands' " (20:5, NIV), God said to him, " 'Now therefore, restore the man's wife; for he is a prophet, and he will pray for you and you shall live' " (20:7).

The prophet of prophets

Moses was the first member of the nation of Israel who was called a prophet. Born to Hebrew parents who lived as slaves in Egypt, he was adopted by Pharaoh's daughter and educated in all the wisdom of Egypt. His training included the religious and legal traditions of the ancient Near East, as well as government service in the greatest empire the world had seen up to that time.

Moses believed himself to be the one to deliver his people from the yoke of slavery, but he failed in his attempt to rescue his people in his own power and had to flee to Midian (see Exodus 2:15). While living in Midian and taking care of the sheep of Jethro, his father-in-law, Moses received the education that prepared him for his future role as the God-sent deliverer of Israel. "While he was living in retirement, the Lord sent His angels to especially instruct him in regard to the future. Here he learned more fully the great lesson of self-control and humility. He kept the flocks of Jethro, and while he was performing his humble duties as a shepherd, God was preparing him to become a spiritual shepherd of His sheep, even of His people Israel" (SR 110).

After forty years in Midian, Moses returned to Egypt with the assurance that God would be with him. He was to lead the children of Israel out of Egypt and into Canaan. The ten plagues in Exodus 7–11 overcame Pharaoh's resistance to letting Israel go, and following a series of miracles along the way, Moses, under God's guidance, led Israel from Egypt to the borders of the Promised Land. There the people listened to the report of the ten spies about the people in Canaan and became so discouraged that they decided to return to Egypt (see Numbers 14:4). This display of unbelief led God to threaten to destroy the people of Israel, prompting Moses to intercede for them. As a consequence of this rebellion, the people of Israel had to wander another thirty-eight years in the wilderness (see Deuteronomy

2:14), and the generation that rebelled against God died out, except for Caleb and Joshua.

The most tragic event in the life of Moses, who was called the most humble man on the earth (see Numbers 12:3), took place at Kadesh-Barnea. There, instead of speaking to the rock, as God had instructed him to do, Moses struck the rock to bring water from it (see Numbers 20:8-12). This single act of disobedience barred him from entering the Promised Land, reminding us that one cherished and unconfessed sin will keep us out of the kingdom. "One cherished sin," says Ellen White, "will, little by little, debase the character, bringing all its nobler powers into subjection to the evil desire" (PP 452).

Shortly before his death, Moses told the Israelites, " 'The LORD your God will raise up for you a Prophet like me from your midst, from your brethren. Him you shall hear' " (Deuteronomy 18:15). This prophecy was initially fulfilled through Joshua and the prophets who followed him. It found its ultimate fulfillment in the appearance of the Messiah, who was the Prophet who would lead God's people from the slavery of sin into the heavenly Canaan.

Many years after Moses' death, when Joshua wrote the closing verses of Deuteronomy, he said, "Since then there has not arisen in Israel a prophet like Moses, whom the LORD knew face to face" (Deuteronomy 34:10). There was no other prophet like Moses until the time of the Messiah who, the book of Hebrews says, was not only greater than any other prophet, including Moses (see Hebrews 3:3), but greater even than the angels (1:4). He was, after all, "God . . . manifested in the flesh" (1 Timothy 3:16).

Prophets and kings

Throughout the time of the monarchy, prophets had the freedom to rebuke kings and princes in the name of the Lord (see 1 Samuel 13:13, 14; 1 Kings 20:41-43). They reminded the rulers that their sovereignty wasn't unlimited, that the Lord's rule and judgment were above the king's rule. The prophets' ability to speak plainly, pointing out the sins of the people and their rulers, was of great importance in the history of Israel. This set them apart from so-called prophets in other nations. "A striking contrast to the prophets' threats of doom, hurled against kings and princes, was the anxiety often shown by Assyrian diviners 'to explain away for their masters' comfort the threatening signs which they cannot deny having observed.' "[6]

The Prophetic Gift

This independence of the biblical prophets made it possible for the prophet Nathan to rebuke King David for his crime against Uriah the Hittite (see 2 Samuel 12:1-13). Nathan's prophetic authority was also the reason why David didn't build the temple (see 7:12-17), and it was Nathan's intervention that secured Solomon's accession to the throne (see 1 Kings 1:11-14).

After the division of the nation of Israel into the northern kingdom, also called Israel, and the southern kingdom, Judah, in 931 B.C., Jeroboam, the first king of Israel, built two centers of worship for his people in the north, one in Bethel and the other in Dan. He reasoned in his heart, " 'If these people go up to offer sacrifices in the house of the LORD at Jerusalem, then the heart of this people will turn back to their lord, Rehoboam king of Judah, and they will kill me and go back to Rehoboam king of Judah' " (1 Kings 12:26, 27). As Jeroboam was officiating as priest at the dedication of the new altar at Bethel, a prophet of God protested, " 'O altar, altar! Thus says the LORD: "Behold, a child, Josiah by name, shall be born to the house of David; and on you he shall sacrifice the priests of the high places who burn incense on you, and men's bones shall be burned on you" ' " (1 Kings 13:2).

This prophecy was fulfilled literally about three hundred years later when Josiah, the king of Judah (639–609 B.C.), demolished the altar at Bethel. "Josiah looked around, and when he saw the tombs that were there on the hillside, he had the bones removed from them and burned on the altar to defile it, in accordance with the word of the LORD proclaimed by the man of God who foretold these things" (2 Kings 23:16, NIV).

When King Ahab and his wife Jezebel introduced the cult of Baal in Israel, the northern kingdom, Elijah and other prophets led the fight against it (see 1 Kings 18; 20:13-43). Jezebel had some of them killed because of their opposition (see 1 Kings 18:4, 13, 22; 19:10-14; 2 Kings 9:7). Then, having failed to persuade one of their citizens, Naboth, to sell them his vineyard, Ahab and Jezebel had him falsely accused and put to death. But no sooner was Naboth dead than the prophet Elijah appeared proclaiming in the name of God, " ' " 'In the place where dogs licked the blood of Naboth, dogs shall lick your blood' " ' " (1 Kings 21:19). This prophecy was fulfilled when, on the day that King Ahab died in battle, "someone washed the chariot at a pool in Samaria, and the dogs licked up his blood while the harlots bathed, according to the word of the LORD which He had spoken" (1 Kings 22:38).

The voice of the prophets was the voice of supreme authority, expressing the viewpoint and will of God. Their words not only rivaled the decisions of the kings and the counsel of the priests, the prophets frequently defied and even condemned the words and deeds of priests, false prophets, princes, and kings (see Isaiah 3:12, 14, 15; Jeremiah 2:26; Micah 3:1-3, 11; Zephaniah 3:4).

Prophetesses in Israel

The official leadership for the worship of God was in the hands of the Aaronic priesthood. Unlike other religions of the ancient Near East, the Hebrew religion had no priestesses. There were, however, prophetesses. Five women in the Old Testament are called "prophetess": Miriam, Deborah, Hulda, Isaiah's wife, and Noadiah. Miriam was Moses' and Aaron's sister (see Exodus 15:20). Deborah was a judge in Israel (see Judges 4:4). Huldah lived in Jerusalem during the time of Josiah (see 2 Kings 22:14). In the case of Isaiah's wife, "prophetess" may have been an honorary title (see Isaiah 8:3).* And Noadiah, whose name means something like "Yahweh has met by appointment," was a false prophetess associated with Tobiah and Sanballat in opposition to Nehemiah (see Nehemiah 6:14).

Together with Moses and Aaron, Miriam was instrumental in leading the Israelites out of Egypt and making them into a new nation. In Micah 6:4, God told the Israelites, " 'I brought you up from the land of Egypt, / I redeemed you from the house of bondage; / And I sent before you Moses, Aaron, and Miriam.' " That she is called a "prophetess" indicates not only that she composed the song that is now part of Scripture (see Exodus 15:21), but also that the Lord spoke to her, something she claims in Numbers 12:2. Ellen White confirmed that Miriam indeed had the prophetic gift: "Aaron and Miriam had occupied a position of high honor and leadership in Israel. Both were endowed with the prophetic gift, and both had been divinely associated with Moses in the deliverance of the Hebrews" (PP 382). According to Jewish tradition, Miriam became the wife of Hur, who with Aaron held up the hands of Moses in the battle with the Amalekites (see Exodus 17:10-12).

Miriam is remembered, primarily, for two things. First, after the miracle of the crossing of the Red Sea and the destruction of the Egyptian army, she

---

* In the ancient Near East, titles were sometimes given to wives or daughters of officials; e.g., in the Mishnah, a priest's wife and daughter were called priestesses.

led the Hebrew women in a song of praise (see Exodus 15:20, 21). This was Miriam's great hour, she was the best known woman in the new nation of Israel, and "in the affections of the people and the honor of Heaven she stood second only to Moses and Aaron" (PP 382).

The second event for which Miriam is remembered is her rebellion against the leadership of Moses (see Numbers 12). The same kind of jealousy that had led to Satan's downfall took hold of Miriam's heart. Because Moses had accepted the counsel of his father-in-law without consulting Aaron and Miriam in the appointment of the seventy elders (see Exodus 18), they felt slighted. "In the organization of the council of elders they felt that their position and authority had been ignored. Miriam and Aaron had never known the weight of care and responsibility which had rested upon Moses; yet because they had been chosen to aid him they regarded themselves as sharing equally with him the burden of leadership, and they regarded the appointment of further assistants as uncalled for" (PP 383).

A second reason for her jealousy was Moses' marriage to Zipporah (see Numbers 12:2). Some scholars think that Moses married the dark-skinned Cushite woman after the death of Zipporah the Midianite (see Exodus 2:15-21). "In Hab. 3:7, however, 'Cushan' and 'Midian' occur in parallelism, which suggests that the terms could be synonymous. Since the peoples of Nubia and Ethiopia were black-skinned, possibly the term was applied to other darker-skinned nomadic peoples like the Midianites."[7]

Miriam may have sinned because of pride in her own race. Perhaps she told Moses that he should have chosen a wife from among his own people. She compounded the problem by making the matter public, which tended to break down Moses' authority among the Israelites. There is a peculiar irony to her punishment. She who had complained about the dark-skinned woman became a leper "as white as snow" (Numbers 12:10). Her "white skin" was anything but healthy and certainly nothing to be proud of. Moses interceded for her with the Lord, and after seven days she was healed of her leprosy. Most likely, the leprosy of her heart departed with the leprosy of her skin. Nothing more is reported of her except her death and burial at Kadesh (see Numbers 20:1).

Deborah, a prophetess and judge in Israel (see Judges 4; 5), must have been an extraordinary woman. In a society dominated by men, she became the political and spiritual leader of a whole nation, something few women achieved in those days.

For twenty years, the Israelites groaned under the yoke of Jabin, king of Hazor. Finally, they remembered their past, turned from their idolatry, and with repentant hearts cried to the Lord for deliverance. And the Lord heard them. However, the deliverer whom God sent wasn't a man, but Deborah, a woman well-known for her piety. She was also known as a prophetess, and in the absence of the usual magistrates, she became a judge for her people, who came to her for counsel and justice.

"The Lord communicated to Deborah His purpose to destroy the enemies of Israel, and bade her send for a man named Barak . . . and make known to him the instructions which she had received. She accordingly sent for Barak, and directed him to assemble ten thousand men of the tribes of Naphtali and Zebulun, and make war upon the armies of King Jabin" (RC 329).

This battle between the Israelites and the Canaanites in the Valley of Jezreel—also called the plain of Megiddo—became a symbol of God's intervention in judgment upon the nations and a symbol for His deliverance of His people (see Joel 3:12-16). Consequently, in the book of Revelation, the final battle between good and evil is called the battle of Armageddon (see Revelation 16:12-16).

Megiddo, from which may come the word *Armageddon* ("mountain of Megiddo"), was on one side of the plain of Jezreel. But it was from a mountain (Mount Tabor) that God had designated previously that Israel proceeded to victory against the host that God had said would be gathered against them in that valley.

Thus, the 144,000 of the Israel of God in the time of the sixth plague, like the 10,000 of Israel of old on the sides of Mount Tabor, are to look to God for deliverance from their oppressors. They are to take their stand upon the mountain of faith and obedience that overlooks the valley of deliverance.

Following the defeat of Jabin's army, Deborah ascribed all praise for the victory to God (see Judges 5:3-5, 13). She refused to accept any glory for herself or Barak. As a "mother in Israel" (Judges 5:7), she continued to watch over the people with maternal care, counseling, and aiding them in their search for justice.

New Testament prophets

The word *prophet,* or *prophets,* appears about 150 times in the New

Testament, mostly in the Gospels (86 times) and in the book of Acts (30 times). In the vast majority of cases in the New Testament, the word *prophet* refers to the Old Testament prophets; only a few times is it used for people actually living in New Testament times.

Among the pre-Christian prophets in the New Testament was Zacharias, who "was filled with the Holy Spirit, and prophesied" (Luke 1:67); his wife, Elizabeth, who also being filled with the Holy Spirit, greeted Mary as the mother of the Messiah (see Luke 1:41-43); and Simon and Anna in the temple (see Luke 2:25-32, 36-38). All of them were pious Jews.

The most prominent pre-Christian prophet in the New Testament was John the Baptist. "Of no [other] prophet is it stated that he was filled with the Holy Ghost from his mother's womb, Lk. 1:15. Other prophets, even though God chose them prior to their birth (Jer. 1:5), were seized by the Spirit and given special tasks only as adults. John stands apart. He is a Spirit-filled prophet from the very first; he is *the* prophet."[8] John the Baptist was not only the forerunner of the Messiah (see Matthew 3:1-3), he was the expected prophet, the promised Elijah (see Matthew 11:14).

Jesus is referred to as a prophet about twenty times. In most cases, it is the people who call Jesus a prophet (see Matthew 21:11; Luke 24:19). In Mark 6:4 and Luke 4:24, however, Jesus by implication identifies Himself as a prophet.

Living prophets in the time of the New Testament are scarce. Apart from the prophets and teachers at Antioch (Barnabas, Simeon who was called Niger, Lucius of Cyrene, Manaen, and Saul, mentioned in Acts 13:1), the only other New Testament prophets mentioned by name are "Judas and Silas" in Acts 15:32 and a prophet by the name of Agabus in Acts 21:10. To this group we should add the four daughters of Philip the evangelist (see Acts 21:9), though we don't know their names. Other nameless prophets are mentioned in Acts 11:27 and in 1 Corinthians 14:29-32.

In Ephesians 4:11, 12, Paul tells us that God has placed apostles, prophets, evangelists, pastors, and teachers in the church "for the equipping of the saints for the work of ministry, for the edifying of the body of Christ." Similarly, in 1 Corinthians 12:28, 29, Paul lists the prophetic gift among other spiritual gifts.

CHAPTER 3

Spiritual Gifts and Counterfeits

On June 19, 1994, the London *Sunday Telegraph* told its readers: " 'British Airways flight 092 took off from Toronto Airport on Thursday evening just as the Holy Spirit was landing on a small building 100 yards from the end of the runway.' "[1] What has happened since then at this church in Toronto has been a source of joy for many but perplexing and even offensive to many others.

A reporter from *Toronto Life Magazine* went to one of the meetings and described what he experienced:

> The man sitting beside me, Dwayne from California, roared like a wounded lion. The woman beside Dwayne started jerking so badly her hands struck her face. People fell like dominoes, collapsing chairs as they plunged to the carpeting. They howled like wolves, brayed like donkeys and—in the case of a young man standing near the sound board—started clucking like a feral chicken. And the tears! Never have I seen people weep so hysterically, as though every hurt they'd ever encountered had risen to the surface and popped like an overheated tar bubble. This was eerie . . . stuff—people were screaming, their bodies jerking unnaturally, their faces contorted with tics.[2]

Many Christians in the charismatic and Pentecostal world believe that the proclamation of the gospel should normally be accompanied by "signs, wonders, and miracles," including the gift of prophecy as it was in New Testament times.

At Pentecost, the early church received the promised power, also called the early or former rain, that enabled the believers to preach the gospel fearlessly and perform many miraculous signs and wonders (see Acts 1:8; 3:1-10; 5:1-12). For the end time, God has promised to pour His Spirit on all flesh (see Joel 2:28, 29). This means "the great work of the gospel is not to close with less manifestation of the power of God than marked its opening. The prophecies which were fulfilled in the outpouring of the former rain at the opening of the gospel are again to be fulfilled in the latter rain at its close" (GC 611, 612).

Referring to that time, Ellen G. White wrote that "servants of God, with their faces lighted up and shining with holy consecration, will hasten from place to place to proclaim the message from heaven. By thousands of voices, all over the earth, the warning will be given. Miracles will be wrought, the sick will be healed, and signs and wonders will follow the believers" (GC 612).

But Christians must beware. In Matthew 24:24, Jesus warned of false christs and prophets. Paul wrote to the Thessalonians, "The coming of the lawless one is according to the working of Satan, with all power, signs, and lying wonders" (2 Thessalonians 2:9). And Ellen White wrote,

> Before the final visitation of God's judgments upon the earth there will be among the people of the Lord such a revival of primitive godliness as has not been witnessed since apostolic times. . . . The enemy of souls desires to hinder this work; and before the time for such a movement shall come, he will endeavor to prevent it by introducing a counterfeit. In those churches which he can bring under his deceptive power he will make it appear that God's special blessing is poured out; there will be manifest what is thought to be great religious interest. Multitudes will exult that God is working marvelously for them, when the work is that of another spirit. Under a religious guise, Satan will seek to extend his influence over the Christian world (GC 464).

Many Christians today are looking for an experience—a manifestation of the presence of God in their lives—and if such an experience is presented by well-known preachers and packaged in the right way, most people are happy to accept it. Could it be that what we see taking place in the Christian world today is the predicted counterfeit? Three modern signs-and-wonders phenomena are speaking in tongues, healing, and prophecy.

Speaking in tongues

At Pentecost, the Holy Spirit enabled the disciples to speak many different languages (see Acts 2:1-6). From that time on, says Ellen White, their language "was pure, simple, and accurate, whether they spoke in their native tongue or in a foreign language" (AA 40).

Linguists have studied modern instances in which people claimed they spoke supernaturally in other tongues—a phenomenon called glossolalia—to find out whether they were speaking an actual language or not. The results have been rather one-sided. Tongues-speakers today do not speak languages; instead, they speak gibberish.

After investigating glossolalia, Professor William Welmes, professor of African languages at UCLA, wrote, "I must report without reservation that my sample does *not* sound like a language structurally. There can be no more than two contrasting vowel sounds, and a most peculiarly restricted set of consonant sounds; these combine into a very few syllable clusters which recur many times in various orders. The consonants and vowels do not all sound like English [the speaker's native language], but the intonation patterns are so completely American English that the total effect is a bit ludicrous."[3]

Similarly, William J. Samarin, professor of linguistics at Toronto University, studied glossolalia extensively for five years. He assessed glossolalia to be "meaningless but phonologically structured human utterance believed by the speaker to be a real language but bearing no systematic resemblance to any natural language, living or dead."[4]

The gift of tongues is viewed today as a wholly mystical ability that somehow operates in a person's spirit but bypasses the mind. For many years Charles and Francis Hunter held seminars, attended by as many as fifty thousand people at a time, in which they taught people how to receive the gift of tongues. Charles Hunter told the people,

> When you pray with your spirit, you do not think of the sounds of the language. Just trust God, but make the sounds when I tell you to.

Spiritual Gifts and Counterfeits

In just a moment when I tell you to, begin loving and praising God by speaking forth a lot of different syllable sounds. At first make the sounds rapidly so you won't try to think as you do in speaking your natural language. . . . Make the sounds loudly at first so you can easily hear what you are saying.[5]

Hunter continually reminded his audience that they weren't supposed to be thinking. " 'The reason some of you don't speak fluently,' " he said, " 'is that you tried to think of the sounds. So when we pray this prayer and you start speaking in your heavenly language, don't try to think. . . . [You] don't have to think in order to pray in the Spirit.' "[6]

This desire to switch off the mind and disconnect from all that is rational is one of the primary characteristics of pagan mystery religions. Yet about 20 percent of all Christians today belong to some tongue-speaking Pentecostal or charismatic church, and if one counts only committed Christians, the percentage is even higher.

Ellen G. White calls the modern tongues "gibberish." In 1864 she wrote, "Some of them have exercises which they call gifts, and say that the Lord has placed them in the church. They have an unmeaning gibberish which they call the unknown tongue, which is unknown not only by man, but by the Lord and all Heaven. Such gifts are manufactured by men and women, aided by the great Deceiver. Fanaticism, false excitement, false talking in tongues, and noisy exercises have been considered gifts which God has placed in the church. Some have been deceived here. The fruits of all this have not been good" (4bSG 153). Nowhere does the Bible teach that the gift of tongues is anything other than human languages.

Healing

During Jesus' three and a half years of ministry, He healed many sick people (Matthew 15:30). After His ascension, He promised His disciples that those who believed would be able to " 'place their hands on [the] sick' " and people would get well (Mark 16:18, NIV). Today, thousands flock to healing services all over the world, and every week, tens of thousands of viewers worldwide watch television preachers conduct healing services. Generally, those seeking healing can be seen standing in line, waiting for the evangelist to touch them. When he does, they fall back like tenpins, and "catchers" behind them lay them out on the floor like fence posts. With its "faith formula" for health, wealth, and prosperity, the Faith Movement has taken many Christian churches by storm.

Kenneth Copeland and Benny Hinn, TV preachers well-known on many continents, are prominent representatives of the Faith Movement, which teaches that the human mind and the tongue contain supernatural power. Psalm 33:9 says, "He spoke, and it was done; / He commanded, and it stood fast." Taking this principle, the Faith Movement teaches that when people speak, expressing their faith in divine laws, their positive thoughts and positive verbal expressions generate a "divine force" that will heal, produce wealth, and bring success.

Most of these so-called healings cannot be verified. Some years ago, W. A. Nolan, a medical doctor, tested the claims of faith healers and then wrote a book called *Healing: A Doctor in Search of a Miracle*. Nolan wrote,

> Search the literature, as I have, and you will find no documented cures by healers of gallstones, heart disease, cancer or any other serious organic disease. Certainly, you'll find patients temporarily relieved of their upset stomachs, their chest pains, their breathing problems; and you will find healers, and believers, who will interpret this interruption of symptoms as evidence that the disease is cured. But when you track the patient down and find out what happened later, you always find the "cure" to have been purely symptomatic and transient. The underlying disease remains.[7]

While this may be true in many cases, it cannot be denied that some genuine healings may take place. The question is, From which power does the healing come? Ellen White predicted, "Wonderful scenes, with which Satan will be closely connected, will soon take place. God's Word declares that Satan will work miracles. He will make people sick, and then will suddenly remove from them his satanic power. They will then be regarded as healed. These works of apparent healing will bring Seventh-day Adventists to the test" (2SM 53).

This statement doesn't mean that every healing must be from Satan, but Christians must be aware of possible counterfeit miracles. Nevertheless, genuine miracles in response to sincere prayers may take place every day.

Prophecy

Seventh-day Adventists believe in the gift of prophecy in the time of the end, but we also believe that everything should be tested by the Word of God. In recent years, a number of modern prophets have appeared in certain charismatic churches. At one time, Metro Vineyard Fellowship, a charismatic church in Kansas City, had three modern prophets who were known as "the Kansas City prophets." The prophecies and messages of these modern prophets were frequently false and often foolish. For example, J. P. Jackson, one of these prophets, "said in one message that God blew up the space shuttle Challenger to teach Americans a lesson, given that there was a teacher on board."[8] And Bob Jones, another Kansas City prophet, predicted "that 1,000 religious leaders would die in 1989 because of their abuse of spiritual gifts."[9] He also spoke of a new breed of humans, "the elect seed," created by God in 1973 to form a super church that would be " 'ten thousand times greater than the church in the book of Acts.' "[10]

These prophets don't believe that they have the same authority as the biblical prophets. They admit they have prophesied falsely. Nevertheless, thousands regard the prophecies these men deliver as messages from God. The pastor of the church actively encourages the members to embrace modern prophecies as God's means of revealing fresh truths to the church.

Evangelical theologians have worked out a whole theology to justify the existence of modern prophets such as these. Wayne Grudem, who teaches at Trinity Evangelical Divinity School, believes that Scripture is verbally inspired. In regard to modern prophets he says, "Prophecy today is *merely human words* reporting what God has brought to mind, while the prophecies that were written down in the Old Testament were men speaking God's *words* to report what God had brought to mind."[11] Therefore, he believes that modern prophets can make mistakes. Bob Jones once said, "If I hit two-thirds of it [in other words, if two-thirds of his prophecies are fulfilled], I am doing pretty good."[12]

Of course, this distinction between thought and verbal inspiration satisfies only those who, unlike Seventh-day Adventists, believe in verbal inspiration.

Pentecostalism and the Seventh-day Adventist Church

What relevance does the charismatic movement with its signs and wonders have for the Seventh-day Adventist Church? Are we in any way affected by it? Unfortunately, we are not immune to what is happening in other churches.

In recent years, a number of congregations in the United States have left the Seventh-day Adventist denomination and become independent churches. In all cases, new worship styles and other charismatic influences were partly responsible for their separation. One Adventist pastor, for example, appointed a Pentecostal pastor to lead the worship praise music. When the conference asked him not to use the Pentecostal worship leader and to change the direction he was taking his church, he refused. Because of his insubordination, his employment was then terminated, but about a hundred people left with him and formed a congregational Seventh-day Adventist church.

Eoin Giller, a Seventh-day Adventist pastor and Bible teacher from Australia, was dismissed from the ministry in America because he began holding healing services and speaking in tongues. He claims to have the gift of healing, the gift of tongues, and the gift of prophecy—no, more than that: he claims to have been given the prophetic office.

In January 1996, Giller and his wife went to Toronto for the second anniversary of the Toronto Blessing. Of his experience he said,

> While we were travelling the Lord told me He was going to reveal my prophetic calling publicly. . . . After Dr. R. T. Kendall's powerful sermon, Dr. Paul Cain stepped to the platform and began to speak words of public prophecy. Dr. Cain is a vindicated prophet of long standing, deeply respected by millions in the Body of Christ. Ella and I were seated near the back of the auditorium in a crowd of 2,500 people. Neither of us had registered in the conference, and Dr. Cain did not know us. Before that large audience, Dr. Cain called for me to stand, recounted our background in Arizona, told me my age when I was first anointed by the Holy Spirit (prior to my fiery baptism in the Spirit), and named Ella. He stated, "Let nothing discourage you or deter you because this is true prophetic gifting that is upon you. You will be known as a prophet of the Lord."[13]

At a meeting of more than a thousand evangelical and Pentecostal/charismatic ministers and members in Rochester, N.Y., Giller saw a Pentecostal minister washing the feet of a young Baptist pastor.

As the two men washed each other's feet, the Spirit of the Lord fell on me in the gallery up in the back of the church. He told me, "This is a wedding, not a foot-washing. Every wedding is made by a third party. You are the third party. As I took Pastor Sheets to England, so I have brought you to America to help make this marriage. Since early this century, the adversary has focused on keeping the Spirit and the Truth separate. These days are over. I am putting the Spirit and the Truth together in My Church. The Evangelicals with the Gospel are to join with the Charismatics in the Spirit. I seek worshippers who will worship Me in Spirit and in truth. Go down and announce this marriage to this church, this city and this nation."

Giller delivered the message, and then, he says,

as I walked off the platform, the Lord said, "Get out of the church." I walked straight out of the building into the night. While I was alone outside, the Lord spent forty minutes giving me specific details about the role He wants the Seventh-day Adventist Church and its leadership to play in the forthcoming marriage. That's when I said to Him, "Lord it ain't [sic] going to work. They'll never do it, they're too proud." Then He said sharply, "You mind your business, and I'll mind Mine! Do what I tell you." In His mercy, the Lord has shown me what will happen if the church leaders fail Him in this momentous hour. The marriage will take place.[14]

Evaluation

In evaluating what is happening in many charismatic churches as well as in some Seventh-day Adventist churches, we need to remember that while the Bible clearly affirms that in the last days God will pour out His Spirit on all people (see Acts 2:17), it also emphatically states, "Beloved, do not believe every spirit, but test the spirits, whether they are of God; because many false prophets have gone out into the world" (1 John 4:1).

• Jesus warned of false prophets: " 'Beware of false prophets, who come to you in sheep's clothing, but inwardly they are ravenous wolves. You will know them by their fruits' " (Matthew 7:15, 16).

- Miracles are not necessarily a proof of God's power: " 'Not everyone who says to Me, "Lord, Lord," shall enter the kingdom of heaven, but he who does the will of My Father in heaven. Many will say to Me in that day, "Lord, Lord, have we not prophesied in Your name, cast out demons in Your name, and done many wonders in Your name?" And then I will declare to them, "I never knew you; depart from Me, you who practice lawlessness!" ' " (Matthew 7:21-23).

- Signs and wonders may be supernatural, but this does not mean they must be from God. " 'False Christs and false prophets will rise and show great signs and wonders to deceive, if possible, even the elect' " (Matthew 24:24).

- Ellen White has warned that in the last days Satan will work miracles: "The man who makes the working of miracles the test of his faith will find that Satan can, through a species of deceptions, perform wonders that will appear to be genuine miracles" (Mar 156).

The fact that this charismatic movement of signs and wonders is sweeping away denominational boundaries and thereby promoting and accelerating the ecumenical idea among Christian churches shouldn't surprise us. More than one hundred years ago, Ellen White wrote, "When the leading churches of the United States, uniting upon such points of doctrine as are held by them in common, shall influence the state to enforce their decrees and to sustain their institutions, then Protestant America will have formed an image to the Roman hierarchy" (GC 445). Before they can influence the state, they must unite. This is what we see happening in the ecumenical movement today.

CHAPTER 4

The Gift of Prophecy and God's Remnant Church

Seventh-day Adventists believe it is their appointed role as the remnant church of prophecy to restore revealed truths that in the course of history were either lost or abandoned. For instance, in worshiping God as Creator-Redeemer they seek to restore the seventh-day Sabbath as the memorial of Creation.

In Scripture, the remnant theme runs from Genesis to Revelation. The earliest reference to a remnant appears in the story of the Flood. Noah and his family were the remnant in the ark (see Genesis 7:23), while the ungodly outside perished. In the time of King Ahab, Elijah thought he was the only true believer left in Israel, but God assured him that there was a remnant of seven thousand who had not bowed their knees to Baal (see 1 Kings 19:18). Amos wrote that Israel would come to an end as a nation but that the Lord might have mercy and leave a remnant (see Amos 5:15). The gospel prophet Isaiah named his son Shear-Jashub, "a remnant shall return" (Isaiah 7:3), predicting the return of a remnant to God (see 10:20-22). And Jeremiah prophesied that the Lord will gather His remnant from the ends of the world, write His law in their hearts, and make a covenant with them (Jeremiah 31:7, 31-34).

In the New Testament, the apostle Paul refers to a remnant in Romans 11:5. The faithful remnant in Paul's day consisted of those among the Jewish people who accepted Jesus as the Messiah and who became the nucleus of the Christian church. In the book of Revelation, a remnant appears in the churches of Thyatira (2:24) and Sardis (3:4) and in chapter 12.

God's faithful remnant was not always a visible remnant. In the days of Elijah, only God knew the faithful in Israel. Similarly, throughout Christian history there has always existed an invisible faithful remnant consisting of people of different religious persuasions. Today also there are faithful members in all Christian churches, including the Roman Catholic Church. They have accepted Christ as their personal Savior, and they are counted as His people. Therefore, in the time of the end, the call is made, " 'Come out of her [Babylon], my people' " (Revelation 18:4). Many of God's people are still in Babylon, but they belong to God's invisible church and at the time of the loud cry of Revelation 18:4, they will come out and join the visible remnant church of God described in Revelation 12:17.

The remnant in Revelation 12

Revelation 12 clearly teaches that God has a remnant church in the time of the end. Verses 1-6 of that chapter picture a woman who gives birth to a royal Man-child and a great red dragon that tries to destroy them both. The woman is a symbol of God's faithful people (see Isaiah 54:5, 6; 2 Corinthians 11:2); the dragon is Satan (see Revelation 12:9); the Man-child is Christ (see Psalm 2:9); and the 1,260 prophetic days refer to the period of papal supremacy from the sixth century to the end of the eighteenth century (538–1798).

Revelation 12:7-12 comprises an interlude explaining where Satan came from. In verse 13, John returns to the story begun in the first six verses of that chapter:

Now when the dragon saw that he had been cast to the earth, he persecuted the woman who gave birth to the male Child. But the woman was given two wings of a great eagle, that she might fly into the wilderness to her place, where she is nourished for a time and times and half a time, from the presence of the serpent. So the serpent spewed water out of his mouth like a flood after the woman, that he might cause her to be carried away by the flood. But the earth helped the woman, and the earth opened its mouth and swallowed up the flood which the dragon had spewed out of his mouth. And the dragon was enraged with the woman, and he went to make war with the rest of her offspring, who keep the commandments of

God and have the testimony of Jesus Christ (verses 13-17).

Verses 13-15 describe in symbolic terms the persecution of the Christian church, first by the Roman Empire and later by the apostate Roman Church. In verse 16, the earth—personified, and representing the newly discovered continent of America—helps the church by providing a safe haven, symbolically swallowing up the persecuting armies (see Revelation 17:15). In the seventeenth century, sending armies across the Atlantic was a difficult undertaking.

Revelation 12:17 places us in a time after the 1,260-day period—in other words, in the nineteenth century. Satan, seeing that he was unable to destroy God's faithful people, is angry with the remnant of the woman's seed—the remnant church.

Identifying marks of the remnant church

Revelation 12 gives two identifying marks of this remnant church: (1) they keep the commandments of God, and (2) they have the testimony of Jesus.*

1. The commandments of God. Whatever commandments we may want to include in this first mark, we must certainly include the Ten Commandments. Thus, the first identifying sign of the remnant church is their loyalty to God's moral law—the Ten Commandments. In other words, the remnant church obeys all of God's ten commandments, including the fourth, the Sabbath commandment. Thus, in Revelation 12:17, God says in effect, "At the end of time I will have a church—the remnant church—that will be recognized by the fact that the members keep the commandments as I have given them in the beginning, including the Sabbath commandment." In the time of the apostles, this wouldn't have been a special sign because all the followers of Christ kept the Sabbath. But today, when most Christians keep Sunday, the Sabbath has indeed become a distinguishing mark.

2. The testimony of Jesus. The second identifying mark is the "testimony of Jesus" (Gr. *marturia Iesou*). This expression occurs six times in the book of Revelation (1:2, 9; 12:17; 19:10 [twice]; 20:4). What does it mean? Two grammatically possible interpretations have been proposed. The first view

---

* Revelation 14:12 contains two other identifying marks—patience and the faith of Jesus.

41

understands "the testimony of Jesus" as a human testimony, or witness, to Christ.[1] From this perspective, the war mentioned in Revelation 12:17 refers to the "persecutions against all individuals of the church who **keep the commandments of God and bear testimony to Jesus.**"[2] The second view understands "the testimony of Jesus" as the self-revelation of Jesus—His own testimony.[3]

Marturia, the Greek word translated "testimony" in Revelation 12:17, occurs twenty-one times in the writings of John. Fourteen times it appears in a grammatical construction (subjective genitive) that expresses the idea that the testimony is the testimony given by the person referred to, not a testimony about that person. (See, for example, John 1:19; 3:11, 32, 33; 5:31.) In his writings, John consistently expressed the idea of a testimony or witness about somebody by using the preposition *peri* ("about, concerning") with the verb *martureo* ("to witness, testify"). For example, John 1:7, "To bear witness of the light" [*martureo* plus *peri*]; 5:31, " 'If I bear witness of Myself' " [*martureo* plus *peri*]; 1 John 5:9, "he has borne witness to his Son" (RSV) [*martureo* plus *peri*].[4]

John's first two usages of the expression "testimony of Jesus" in Revelation harmonize with this observation and set the pattern for later usages in the book. In Revelation 1:1, 2, the introduction to the book of Revelation, John sets forth the source—God, and the content of the book—the revelation of Jesus Christ. Verse 2 tells us that John bore witness to "the word of God, and to the testimony of Jesus Christ."

"The word of God" is commonly understood to refer to what God says. Consequently, "the testimony of Jesus," which stands in parallel to "the word of God," must mean the testimony that Jesus gives. How did Jesus testify? While here on earth, He testified in person to the people in Palestine. After His ascension, He spoke through His prophets.

In Revelation 1:9, John introduces himself and states his credentials. He says he is on the Isle of Patmos "for the word of God and for the testimony of Jesus Christ." Again, the parallelism between the "word of God" and "the testimony of Jesus" is clear. In John's time "the word of God" meant the Old Testament, and the "testimony of Jesus" meant what Jesus had said in the Gospels and through His prophets, such as Peter and Paul. The "word of God" and the "testimony of Jesus" describe the content of the preaching of John for which he was banished. In Revelation 19:10, John explains that " 'the testimony of Jesus is the spirit of prophecy.' "

The spirit of prophecy

What is "the spirit of prophecy"? This phrase occurs only once in the Bible—only in this text. The closest parallel to it in the Bible is found in 1 Corinthians 12:8-10. There Paul refers to the Holy Spirit, who gives the gift of prophecy among other gifts. The person who receives this gift is called a prophet (see 12:28; Ephesians 4:11). Just as in 1 Corinthians 12:28, where those who have the gift of prophecy (verse 10) are called prophets, so in Revelation 22:8, 9, those who have the Spirit of prophecy (compare 19:10) are called prophets. The parallelism between the two texts (Revelation 19:10 and 22:8, 9) is significant:

19:10	22:8, 9
And I fell at his feet	I fell down to worship before the feet
to worship him.	of the angel who showed me these things.
But he said to me,	Then he said to me,
"See that you do not do that!	"See that you do not do that.
I am your fellow servant,	For I am your fellow servant,
and of your brethren who have	and of your brethren the prophets,
the testimony of Jesus.	and of those who keep the words
Worship God! For the testimony	of this book. Worship God."
of Jesus is the spirit of prophecy."	

The situation in both passages is the same. John falls at the feet of the angel to worship him. The angel's responses are almost identical, yet the difference is significant. In 19:10, the "brethren" are identified by the phrase "who have the testimony of Jesus." In 22:9, these brethren are simply called "prophets." If the Protestant principle of interpreting Scripture by Scripture means anything, this comparison must lead to the conclusion that "the spirit of prophecy" in 19:10 is not the possession of all church members in general but only of those whom God has called to be prophets.

This interpretation is not purely an Adventist one, as can be seen from the writings of other scholars. The Lutheran scholar Hermann Strathmann, for example, says, "According to the parallel 22:9 the brothers referred to are not believers in general but the prophets. Here, too, they are characterised as such. This is the point of v. 10c. If they have the *marturia Iesou* [testimony of Jesus], they have the spirit of prophecy, i.e., they are prophets, and as such they stand alongside the divine, who is himself a prophet, like the angel, who simply stands in the service of the *marturia Iesou* (cf. 1:1)."[5]

Similarly, James Moffat explains, " 'for the testimony . . . of . . . Jesus is . . . the spirit of prophecy.' This prose marginal comment . . . specifically defines the brethren who hold the testimony of Jesus as possessors of prophetic inspiration. The testimony of Jesus is practically equivalent to Jesus testifying."[6]

The witness of the Targums

The Jewish readers in John's day knew what the expression "Spirit of prophecy" meant. They would have understood the expression as a reference to the Holy Spirit, who imparts the prophetic gift to God's messengers. Rabbinic Judaism equated the Old Testament expressions "Holy Spirit," "Spirit of God," and "Spirit of Yahweh" with "the Spirit of prophecy," as we can see in the frequent occurrence of this term in the Targums (written translations of the Old Testament into Aramaic):

> Thereupon the Pharaoh said to his servants, "Can we find a man like this in whom there is *the Spirit of prophecy from before the Lord?*"[7] (Gen. 41:38).

> Whereupon the Lord *revealed Himself* in a cloud and spoke *with* him, and *increased* <some of> the *spirit* that was upon him and placed <it> upon the seventy elders; and when *the spirit of prophecy* rested upon them, they <began> prophesying without *ceasing*. Now two men had remained behind in the camp—one's name was Eldad; the other's name was Medad, yet *the spirit of prophecy* rested upon them though they were listed <among the elders>, but they had not gone out of the Tent and prophesied in the camp [Num. 11:25, 26].

> Then the Lord said to Moses, "Take Joshua, son of Nun, a man who has within himself *the spirit of prophecy,* and lay your hand on him"[8] (Num. 27:18).

Sometimes the term *Spirit of prophecy* refers simply to the Holy Spirit, but in many cases it refers to the gift of prophecy given by the Holy Spirit, as is shown by the context of the standard Hebrew text of the Old Testament, called the Masoretic text (MT). Commenting on the expression "Spirit of prophecy" in the Targums, J. P. Schäfer says,

> An examination of the verses where TO [Targum Onkelos] uses the term "Spirit of prophecy" shows that in almost all cases there is a direct relationship to the prophecy in the biblical context. The translation "Spirit of prophecy," although not in the strictest sense literal, is almost always stipulated through the MT (Gen. 41:38—Joseph had the "Spirit of prophecy" because he was able to interpret Pharaoh's dream; Num. 11:25—The Spirit that settled on the seventy Elders, according to the MT, brought about "prophesying"; Num. 24:2—Bileam prophesied concerning Israel). In other words, the term "Spirit of prophecy" describes a clearly delineated situation, namely the Holy Spirit sent from God who imparts the prophetic gift to man.[9]

F. F. Bruce came to the same conclusion:

> The expression "the Spirit of prophecy" is current in post-biblical Judaism: it is used, for example, in a Targumic circumlocution for the Spirit of Yahweh which comes upon this or that prophet. Thus the Targum of Jonathan renders the opening words of Isa. 61:1 as "The Spirit of prophecy from before the Lord God is upon me." The thought expressed in Rev. 19:10 is not dissimilar to that already quoted from 1 Pet. 1:11 where "the Spirit of Christ" is said to have borne advanced testimony in the Old Testament prophets. There too Jesus is the theme of the witness borne by the prophetic Spirit; the prophets did not know who the person or what the time would be, but at last the secret is out: the person is Jesus; the time is now.
>
> In Rev. 19:10, however, it is through *Christian* prophets that the Spirit of prophecy bears witness. What the prophets of pre-Christian days foretold is proclaimed as an accomplished fact by the prophets of the new age, among whom John occupies a leading place.[10]

Returning to Revelation 12:17, we can say that "the rest of her offspring [the end-time remnant of God's people] . . . keep the commandments of

God and have the testimony of Jesus Christ," which is the Spirit of prophecy, or the prophetic gift. This interpretation is strengthened by a study of the Greek word *echo*, meaning "to have." This word indicates possession. They have a gift of God—the prophetic gift. If the testimony of Jesus were our testimony about Jesus, John would have written something like this: "They keep the commandments of God and testify about Jesus," or, "they bear testimony to Jesus." But the Greek work *echo* is never used in the sense "to bear a witness."[11]

In summary, we can say that the remnant church, which according to prophecy exists after the 1,260-day period (in other words, after 1798), has two specific identifying marks: (1) they keep the commandments of God, including the Sabbath command as God has given it; and (2) they have the testimony of Jesus, which is the Spirit of prophecy, or the prophetic gift in their midst.

The Seventh-day Adventist Church

From its very inception in 1863, the Seventh-day Adventist Church has always claimed these identifying signs for itself. As Adventists we proclaim

George I. Butler (1834–1918)

the Ten Commandments, including the Sabbath; and we believe that as a church we have the testimony of Jesus—that is, that God manifested Himself in the life and work of Ellen G. White. Thus, the Seventh-day Adventist Church is a church prophetically foreseen, not just one more church among many. God has called this church into existence for a very specific purpose—to proclaim the three angels' messages.

Our pioneers were quite certain that the Seventh-day Adventist Church is the remnant church of Revelation 12:17. In an article entitled "Visions and Prophecy," G. I. Butler, General Conference president from 1871 to 1888, asked,

Is there then no people in whom these conditions combine in these last days? We believe they truly do in Seventh-day Adventists.

They have everywhere claimed to be the "remnant" church for the last twenty-five years. . . . Do they keep the commandments of God? Everyone knowing anything about this people can answer that this is the most important part of their faith. . . .

In regard to the Spirit of prophecy, it is a remarkable fact that from the first of their existence as a people, S. D. Adventists have claimed that it has been in active exercise among them.[12]

Ellen White firmly believed that Seventh-day Adventists are God's remnant church and that Revelation 12:17 applies to them. Seventh-day Adventists "are God's representatives upon the earth" (2T 452). "We have the commandments of God and the testimony of Jesus Christ, which is the Spirit of prophecy" (TM 114). And she counseled, "Let all be careful not to make an outcry against the only people who are fulfilling the description given of the remnant people

White family (Ellen, Willie, James, and Edson)

who keep the commandments of God and have faith in Jesus, who are exalting the standard of righteousness in these last days" (TM 58).

As Seventh-day Adventists, we are members of God's remnant church. However, this identification with the remnant church doesn't accord us an exclusive status with God. Salvation isn't guaranteed through membership in any church—we are saved as individuals, not as a church. But being a part of God's remnant church means that we have access to God's special gift, the Spirit of prophecy, and we have the privilege of participating in the proclamation of God's special end-time message, the three angels' messages, to the world.

The prophetic origin of the Adventist movement and God's gracious guidance through the prophetic gift of Ellen White should make us more aware of the responsibility we have as the remnant church, and it should spur us on to finish the work God has given us to do.

A Short Biography of Ellen G. White

1827 Ellen Gould Harmon was born on November 26 in Gorham, Maine.

1840 Ellen and other members of her family heard William Miller lecturing in Portland and accepted his views that Christ would return to earth about the year 1843.

1844 One morning in December 1844, following the Great Disappointment, Ellen Harmon experienced her first vision, in which she witnessed a representation of the travels of the Adventist people to the City of God.

1846 Early in 1845, Ellen met James White, an Adventist preacher then twenty-three years of age. They were married August 30, 1846. The marriage was blessed with four children: Henry (b. 1847, he died at the age of sixteen); Edson (1849); Willie (1854); John Herbert (1860; he died after three months).

1851 James White published Mrs. White's first pamphlet, titled *A Sketch of the Christian Experience and Views of Ellen G. White*.

1858 At Lovett's Grove, Ohio, Mrs. White had a two-hour vision in which she saw events in the great conflict between Christ and Satan.

1863 In Otsego, Michigan, Mrs. White received a comprehensive vision concerning health reform.

1876 At Groveland, Massachusetts, on Sunday, August 27, Ellen White addressed between fifteen and twenty thousand persons without a microphone. Her clear voice could be heard by all.

1881 James White died at the age of sixty. Ellen White was a widow for thirty-four years.

1885 From August 1885 to August 1887, Ellen White lived in Basel, Switzerland. From there she made repeated trips throughout Europe.

1891 Mrs. White spent the years between 1891 and 1900 in Australia supporting the developing work there.

1900 Following her return from Australia, she settled at St. Helena, California, and focused on the publication of books and articles for the church.

1915 Ellen White died on July 16 at the age of eighty-seven. Today, her literary productions amount to about 100,000 pages.

CHAPTER 5

The Inspiration of the Prophets

What is inspiration? An orchestra can give an inspired performance. Artists can be inspired to write music or paint a picture; and athletes may be inspired by their striving for Olympic gold. When used in these contexts, the word *inspired* means something quite different from what it means when used of the Bible. In the world of arts, inspiration refers to a state of creative fervor preceding the composition of a work. In the Bible, it describes the way the Holy Spirit made sure that the biblical writers correctly conveyed God's messages to His people.

Athletes may be inspired or motivated to win gold. Inspiration in Scripture, however, was never something prophets desired, nor did it motivate them to strive for glory, honor, or acceptance. For many, it was a painful experience. Jeremiah complained, "Lord, you deceived me, and I was deceived; / you overpowered me and prevailed" (Jeremiah 20:7, NIV). It seems that he didn't at all enjoy being a prophet of the Lord.

In 2 Timothy 3:16, the apostle Paul wrote, "All scripture is inspired by God" (RSV). Thus, the inspiration of the Bible is clearly a teaching found in Scripture itself. The Old Testament writers often claim to be recording the very words of God, making such statements as "God spoke to Moses and said to him . . ." (Exodus 6:2); " 'The Spirit of the Lord spoke by me, / And His word was on my tongue' " (2 Samuel 23:2); "The word of the Lord came to me, saying . . ." (Jeremiah 2:1); "God said to . . ." (Hosea 1:6); etc. Some people have attempted to count these and similar statements and have come up with more than two thousand such claims of inspiration in the Old Testament alone.[1]

Revelation, inspiration, and illumination

Before proceeding, we need to clarify some terms. While the distinction between inspiration and revelation is not clear-cut, the word *revelation* refers primarily to God's disclosure of truth through words, acts, or any other means, but most fully in the person of Jesus Christ. It refers primarily to the content of truth—the subject matter that is communicated to the prophet. For example, in Daniel 7, the revelation is what Daniel saw.

The term *inspiration*, on the other hand, describes primarily the way God communicates His truth—the method of communication between God and human beings. At times, God used visions and dreams (see Numbers 12:6). At other times, He spoke face to face (see verses 7, 8) or simply guided the writers in some way through the Holy Spirit so that what they wrote was in harmony with His will. Thus the apostle Peter declared, "Prophecy never came by the will of man, but holy men of God spoke as they were moved by the Holy Spirit" (2 Peter 1:21). The word *moved* (Gr. *phero*) is used in Acts 2:2 for the "rushing [*phero*] mighty wind" that descended on the believers at Pentecost. Acts 27:15 refers to a ship that was driven (*phero*) along by the wind, making the sailors unable to steer or control it. So, in 2 Peter 1:21, the use of the word *phero* implies that the biblical writers were borne along by the Spirit as a ship is borne along by the wind. They were under His control.

The third word that needs a brief explanation is the word *illumination*. Illumination is the enlightenment the Holy Spirit provides to help us understand God's Word. While revelation and inspiration affect the biblical authors, illumination affects us as readers. Paul wrote, "The man without the Spirit does not accept the things that come from the Spirit of God, for they are foolishness to him, and he cannot understand them, because they are spiritually discerned" (1 Corinthians 2:14, NIV). In other words, the reader and interpreter of the Scriptures must be led by the same Spirit that inspired the Scriptures. Without the enlightenment of the Holy Spirit, we cannot interpret the Bible correctly, for He alone enables the believer to understand and apply the Scripture. So, any study of the Word of God should begin with a prayer for the Holy Spirit's guidance and illumination.

Models of the inspiration of the Bible

Many evangelical Christians consider the Bible to be verbally inspired and therefore both infallible and inerrant. As W. Elwell explains, "Inerrancy is the view that when all the facts become known, they will demonstrate that the Bible in its original autographs and correctly interpreted is entirely true and never false in all it affirms, whether that relates to doctrine or ethics or to the social, physical, or life sciences."[2]

Although Seventh-day Adventists have a high view of Scripture, they have never subscribed to verbal inerrancy. As Ellen White explained,

> The Bible is written by inspired men, but it is not God's mode of thought and expression. It is that of humanity. God, as a writer, is not represented. Men will often say such an expression is not like God. But God has not put Himself in words, in logic, in rhetoric, on trial in the Bible. The writers of the Bible were God's penmen, not His pen. Look at the different writers.
>
> It is not the words of the Bible that are inspired, but the men that were inspired. Inspiration acts not on the man's words or his expressions but on the man himself, who, under the influence of the Holy Ghost, is imbued with thoughts. But the words receive the impress of the individual mind. The divine mind is diffused. The divine mind and will is combined with the human mind and will; thus the utterances of the man are the word of God (1SM 21).

Seventh-day Adventists, therefore, have avoided the term *verbal inspiration* and have generally preferred the term *thought inspiration*. This does not mean that the words of the Bible aren't trustworthy or important. On the contrary, both thoughts and words were involved in the inspiration process. The authors of Scripture received God's messages in visual or verbal form, and they conveyed these messages as best as they could in written form, frequently expressing the thoughts in the very words that they heard God or the angels speak. So Ellen White stated, "I take the Bible just as it is, as the Inspired Word" (1SM 17).

We might further describe biblical inspiration in terms of two models. Most Adventists know and understand the prophetic model of inspiration. It simply means that God communicated with His prophets through (1) dreams and visions (see Numbers 12:6; Isaiah 1:1; Ezekiel 1:1; Daniel 7:1;

Amos 1:1); (2) direct speech (see Genesis 12:1; Exodus 3:4-6); or (3) angels (see Daniel 8:15, 16; 9:21).

In Jeremiah 36:2, the prophet is told, " 'Take a scroll of a book and write on it all the words that I have spoken to you against Israel, against Judah, and against all the nations, from the day I spoke to you, from the days of Josiah even to this day.' " What God said against Israel, Judah, and the nations fills almost the whole book of Jeremiah. It is hardly likely that, on his own, Jeremiah could have remembered everything the Lord had told him over the previous twenty years.* The Holy Spirit must have brought to his mind what he had been told, and the same Spirit also guided him in writing it down, because the end product of what he dictated to his secretary Baruch is called "the words of the Lord" (verse 11). "The experience of Jeremiah indicates that the prophets did not write their books as if they were mere copyists. They were fully involved, while moved and guided by the Spirit, in their writing."[3]

Not all the books of the Bible were written by prophets on the basis of dreams and visions, however. Some books were written under a different model of inspiration. The Gospel of Luke provides a fitting illustration of this model. In his introduction Luke wrote, "Inasmuch as many have taken in hand to set in order a narrative of those things which have been fulfilled among us, just as those who from the beginning were eyewitnesses and ministers of the word delivered them to us, it seemed good to me also, having had perfect understanding of all things from the very first, to write to you an orderly account, most excellent Theophilus, that you may know the certainty of those things in which you were instructed" (Luke 1:1-4).

Nowhere in his Gospel does Luke claim to have had dreams or visions, nor was he an eyewitness of the life of Christ. So, how did he write the Gospel that later became part of the New Testament? In his introduction he mentions other accounts of the life of Christ with which he was obviously familiar. He refers to eyewitnesses, some of whom he probably met and interviewed. The apostles, the seventy disciples, the women who attended Jesus, and members of Jesus' family had been eyewitnesses of Jesus' life and had heard His teachings. Luke may not have had personal interviews with them all, but everything that he records in his Gospel he received in some way from others.

---

* Jeremiah was called to be a prophet in the year 626 B.C. (see Jeremiah 1:2), and the fourth year of Jehoiakim (36:1) was the year 605 B.C.

The Inspiration of the Prophets

Luke also mentions "ministers of the word" (*huperetai* in Greek). Who were these people? George Rice believes that they were individuals who performed a special function in the early church. "They were specially chosen to memorize the sermons, parables, and deeds of Jesus. Their responsibility was to repeat from memory what the Lord said and did, and possibly to interpret their meaning."[4] Luke identifies John Mark as one of these *huperetai* in Acts 13:5.

From Luke's introductory statement we can infer that he gathered reports of Jesus' life, interviewed eyewitnesses, collected material, and read books, and the Holy Spirit led him in selecting what to write. Luke arranged the events in the order in which he wanted to present them to Theophilus, a man of high rank in the Roman world of the day. Thus in the book of Luke, we find what may be called "the research model of inspiration." In this model the Holy Spirit guides writers in their research, reading, and interviews, and then He directs them in the selection and presentation of their material. From the time of the early church onward, Christians believed that the Holy Spirit guided Luke in the selection of the material and ensured that what he wrote down was in harmony with the historical events and with God's will. Ellen White has an interesting comment on this point. She wrote, "God has been pleased to communicate His truth to the world by human agencies, and He Himself, by His Holy Spirit, qualified men and enabled them to do this work. He guided the mind in the selection of what to speak and what to write" (GC vi).

Other books most likely written under this model are 1 and 2 Kings and 1 and 2 Chronicles. At times the authors of these books used existing sources, such as court records (see 2 Chronicles 35:4), chronicles (see 1 Chronicles 27:24), histories (see 2 Chronicles 27:7), and books by other prophets (see 1 Kings 11:41; 2 Kings 14:28; 1 Chronicles 29:29). Nevertheless, as the authors studied and composed, the Holy Spirit guided their minds in the selection of what sources to use and what to write.

Some books may have been written under both models of inspiration. For example, we find hints of genealogical tables that Moses consulted in writing the book of Genesis (see Genesis 5:1; 6:9; 10:1; 11:10; etc.). Yet, we know that Moses was also the recipient of many visions and verbal communications from God. Ellen White says that most of the content of the book of Genesis was revealed to Moses while he was in Midian taking care of his father-in-law's herds and flocks (see PP 251).

Some of Paul's letters might also fall into this category. He received visions (see 2 Corinthians 12:1-7), but he also received information from church

53

members that he incorporated into his letters (see 1 Corinthians 1:10, 11). At times he also quoted from pagan authors. For example, the saying "Bad company corrupts good character" (see 1 Corinthians 15:33, NIV) is a quote from the Greek poet Menander (343–280 B.C.), and the Cretan "prophet" whom he cites in Titus 1:12 was most likely Epimenides.

Although the biblical authors used different sources in addition to revelations from heaven, the end product of this cooperative effort between God and man was the Word of God, because all the writing was done under the supervision of the Holy Spirit.

The inspiration of Ellen G. White

John N. Loughborough (1832–1924)

Scripture doesn't recognize degrees of inspiration. One prophet can't be only 50 percent inspired and another prophet 80 percent inspired. People are either inspired or uninspired. Therefore, we must conclude that the Holy Spirit who inspired the biblical authors also inspired Ellen White to the same degree.

During the seventy years of her ministry, Ellen White received about two thousand visions and dreams. She received her first vision late in 1844 and her last one on March 3, 1915. During the first forty years of her ministry, she received many open visions—in other words, public visions during which it was apparent to people around her that she was in vision. According to J. N. Loughborough, who witnessed about fifty such visions, her last public vision occurred at the 1884 Oregon camp meeting.[5]

Why did the open visions cease in 1884? A little study reveals that God launched the Christian church with many supernatural phenomena. At Pentecost, the appearance of tongues caused quite a stir in the community (see Acts 2:5-13). Peter and John healed a lame man at the temple gate, and the people were amazed (see Acts 3:6-10). Ananias and Sapphira were slain (see Acts 5:5, 10), and Dorcas was raised from the dead (see Acts 9:40-42). But once the church was established, these manifestations diminished. God still worked miracles, but these public demonstrations of His power were no longer needed.

So also in the early Seventh-day Adventist Church—the supernatural, visible manifestations diminished as the church became established and the prophet became accepted.

Is everything Ellen White ever wrote inspired by God? No. She herself explained why not:

> There are times when common things must be stated, common thoughts must occupy the mind, common letters must be written and information given that has passed from one to another of the workers. Such words, such information, are not given under the special inspiration of the Spirit of God. Questions are asked at times that are not upon religious subjects at all, and these questions must be answered. We converse about houses and lands, trades to be made, and locations for our institutions, their advantages and disadvantages (1SM 39).

Just like the biblical prophets, Ellen White had to deal with issues and questions that had nothing to do with her prophetic gift. What she wrote or said in regard to these matters, therefore, was not inspired. Note also what she said in a letter she wrote in 1906 to Dr. Paulson, founder and director of the Hinsdale Sanatorium: "In your letter you speak of your early training to have implicit faith in the testimonies and say, 'I was led to conclude and most firmly believe that *every* word that you ever spoke in public or private, that every letter you wrote under *any* and *all* circumstances, was as inspired as the Ten Commandments.'

"My brother, you have studied my writings diligently, and you have never found that I have made any such claims, neither will you find that the pioneers in our cause ever made such claims" (1SM 24).

On the other hand, belief in Ellen White's inspiration means by implication belief that what she declared to be from God must be accepted as such. As F. M. Wilcox, who was for many years the editor of the *Review and Herald* and who knew her personally, said, "We must believe that what she gave, by either voice or pen, in printed page or through the medium of correspondence, *as the messages of God,* was true to this representation. We must accept her statement as true relative to this, or else reject altogether her call to the prophetic office."[6]

In regard to the books that she wrote, she said, "Sister White is not the originator of these books. They contain the instruction that during her lifework God has been giving her. They contain the precious, comforting light that God has graciously given His servant to be given to the world" (CM 125). She said the same about her letters and articles: " 'In these letters which I write, in the testimonies I bear, I am presenting to you that which the Lord has presented to me. I do not write one article in the paper expressing merely my own ideas. They are what God has opened before me in vision—the precious rays of light shining from the throne' " (1SM 29).

The human element in her writings

The fact that Ellen White claimed not to express her own ideas but that which God had shown her doesn't mean that everything she wrote for the church came to her via a heavenly pipeline. What she was shown in the visions she had to write down in her own words. And when she was shown historical scenes that were part of the great controversy, she had to go to history books to find out the names of the places and the dates of the events that she had seen. Consequently, she wrote in the introduction to the book *The Great Controversy*, "In some cases where a historian has so grouped together events as to afford, in brief, a comprehensive view of the subject, or has summarized details in a convenient manner, his words have been quoted" (GC xii). Today we know that she used material from books written by other authors in many of her books. This shouldn't surprise us. Like Moses, Paul, and other biblical authors, she received dreams and visions from God, but she also had to do research before she could write out many of God's messages.

Like the biblical authors, Ellen White at times made mistakes in regard to historical matters. In the Bible we find that Matthew mistakenly wrote "Jeremiah" instead of "Zechariah" (see Matthew 27:9), and Stephen (or Luke) confused the names of Abraham and Jacob in Acts 7:16 (cf. Genesis 23:10-16; 33:19). Because these details weren't important to the message, God didn't intervene to correct them. Similarly, in the writings of Ellen White, one can find details that may not be historically correct. When such things were pointed out to her, she was quite willing to correct them. For example, in her description of the St. Bartholomew Massacre in France in

1572, she followed Wylie's *History of Protestantism* and wrote in the 1888 edition of *The Great Controversy*, "The great bell of the palace, tolling at dead of night, was a signal for the slaughter" (GC [1888] 272). When it was pointed out to her that many subsequent historians believed it was not the palace bell but the bell of the church of St. Germain that gave the signal for the slaughter, she changed the sentence to read, "A bell, tolling at dead of night, was a signal for the slaughter" (GC [1911] 272).

In 1912, her son W. C. White wrote to an inquirer, "Mother has never wished our brethren to treat them [her writings] as authority regarding details of history or historical dates."[7] In the same letter W. C. White said, "When writing out the chapters for *Great Controversy,* she sometimes gave a partial description of an important historical event, and when her copyist who was preparing the manuscripts for the printer, made inquiry regarding time and place, Mother would say that those things are recorded by conscientious histo-

William C. White (1854–1937)

rians. Let the dates used by those historians be inserted" (3SM 447). And even conscientious historians can be mistaken. (However, this doesn't mean we can ignore everything she wrote about history.)

It is important to remember that such minor inaccuracies don't change the message. That's why God didn't think He must intervene supernaturally.

CHAPTER 6

Testing the Prophets

On the basis of Scripture and the evidence of supernatural interventions, as long as the Seventh-day Adventist Church has existed, it has officially recognized the presence of the prophetic gift in the life and ministry of Mrs. Ellen G. White. Fundamental Belief number 18, voted in 1980 at the General Conference in Dallas, states, "One of the gifts of the Holy Spirit is prophecy. This gift is an identifying mark of the remnant church and was manifested in the ministry of Ellen. G. White. As the Lord's messenger, her writings are a continuing and authoritative source of truth which provide for the church comfort, guidance, instruction, and correction. They also make clear that the Bible is the standard by which all teaching and experience must be tested. (Joel 2:28, 29; Acts 2:14-21; Heb. 1:1-3; Rev. 12:17; 19:10)."[1]

Ellen White never called herself a prophetess. In 1905 she wrote, "Others have called me a prophetess, but I have never assumed that title. I have not felt that it was my duty thus to designate myself" (1SM 36). And a year later she said, "To claim to be a prophetess is something that I have never done. If others call me by that name, I have no controversy with them" (1SM 34). The reason she said this was twofold: (1) "Those who boldly assume that they are prophets in this our day are often a reproach to the cause of Christ," and (2) "My work includes much more than this name signifies. I regard myself as a messenger, entrusted by the Lord with messages for His people" (1SM 36).

Elder A. G. Daniells, who worked for many years side by side with Ellen White, stated, "In recognizing an organized, orderly church as Christ's body on earth, and in arousing that church to world-wide missionary activity, and in setting in operation efficient methods of labor, Mrs. White has made a record in harmony with the prophets of God whose lives are recorded and whose works are preserved in the Scriptures for our guidance."[2]

Dreams and visions

In the ancient Near East, dreams and oracles played an important role in the lives of the people. The royal courts of Mesopotamia and Egypt had among their wise men those who interpreted dreams professionally. The ancient Greeks went to the oracle of Delphi to learn the future through the wisdom of Apollo. However, with few exceptions—such as Nebuchadnezzar's dream (see Daniel 2)—such dreams and oracles were not divine communications.

"The multitude of dreams arise from the common things of life, with which the Spirit of God has nothing to do. There are also false dreams, as well as false visions, which are inspired by the spirit of Satan. But dreams from the Lord are classed in the word of God with visions and are as truly the fruits of the spirit of prophecy as visions. Such dreams, taking into the account the persons who have them and the circumstances under which they are given, contain their own proofs of their genuineness" (1T 569, 570).

In Scripture, genuine prophets received prophetic dreams and visions. In Numbers 12:6, God told Aaron and Miriam, who were questioning Moses' authority, " 'Hear now My words: / If there is a prophet among you, / I, the LORD, make Myself known to him in a vision; / I speak to him in a dream.' " (See also Genesis 37:5; 1 Kings 3:5; Isaiah 1:1; Daniel 8:1; Acts 9:10; 10:17; etc.). During her seventy-year ministry, Ellen G. White received approximately two thousand visions and prophetic dreams.

About her state while in vision, she wrote, "When the Lord sees fit to give a vision, I am taken into the presence of Jesus and angels, and am entirely lost to earthly things. I can see no farther than the angel directs me. My attention is often directed to scenes transpiring upon earth. . . .

"After I come out of vision I do not at once remember all that I have seen, and the matter is not so clear before me until I write, then the scene rises before me as was presented in vision, and I can write with freedom" (1SM 36).

Certain physical phenomena accompanied Mrs. White's visions—she didn't breathe, she had supernatural strength (no one could move or restrain her limbs), and she was unconscious of her surroundings. Dr. Lord, a physician who examined her during a vision she received in February 1857, stated, " ' "Her heart beats, but there is no breath. There is life, but no action of the lungs; I cannot account for this condition." ' "3

Agreement with the Bible

What a prophet claims to have received from God must be in harmony with the rest of God's Word, because God doesn't contradict Himself (see Psalm 15:4; Malachi 3:6). Isaiah wrote concerning claimants of supernatural gifts, "To the law and to the testimony! If they do not speak according to this word, it is because there is no light in them" (Isaiah 8:20). The "law" (Heb. *torah*) refers generally to God's revealed will but specifically to the books of Moses, and the "testimony" (Heb. *te'udah*) refers to the messages of the prophets.

Every true prophet has made the writings of previous prophets the benchmark for his or her own ministry. The same is true for Ellen G. White. She constantly quoted and referred to the biblical text. Although she wasn't a trained theologian and she didn't write an exegetical commentary on the Bible, her messages are in harmony with the messages of Scripture.

Some people have claimed that in a number of cases she contradicts the Bible, but a careful investigation of each of these claims shows that they simply aren't true. For example, critics sometimes claim that Ellen White contradicts the Bible because she taught that forgiven sins are not blotted out until the time of the final judgment. In the chapter on the investigative judgment, Ellen White wrote, "All who have truly repented of sin, and by faith claimed the blood of Christ as their atoning sacrifice, have had pardon entered against their names in the books of Heaven; as they have become partakers of the righteousness of Christ, and their characters are found to be in harmony with the law of God, their sins will be blotted out, and they themselves will be accounted worthy of eternal life" (GC 483).

However, critics claim that the Bible teaches that sins are blotted out when they are forgiven, and the critics refer people to Isaiah 43:25, Jeremiah 31:34, Micah 7:19, and Hebrews 8:12. But none of the texts listed tells when the blotting out takes place. In Old Testament times, sins were forgiven immediately, but they remained in the sanctuary until the Day of

Atonement. Today, when sinners come to Christ and confess their sins, they are forgiven completely. Their sins are placed upon Jesus, who has become sinners' Substitute and Surety. And God, in return, "places the obedience of his Son to the sinner's account. Christ's righteousness is accepted in place of man's failure, and God receives, pardons, justifies, the repentant, believing soul, treats him as though he were righteous, and loves him as he loves his Son" (RH Nov. 4, 1890).

But sins are not blotted out immediately. If a righteous man should turn away from God, the book of remembrance, in which all his good deeds were recorded, is not taken into account in the judgment. He is rewarded according to his long catalogue of sins (see Ezekiel 18:24). Not only are sins he has not repented of charged against him, but all those also for which he had earlier obtained pardon. When a man separates himself from God, he rejects His pardoning love and is consequently "in the same condition as before he was forgiven. He has denied his repentance, and his sins are upon him as if he had not repented" (COL 251).

The parable of the unforgiving servant in Matthew 18:21-35 clearly teaches this. The master forgave his servant a great debt; but when this same servant threw his fellow servant who owed him only a little into jail, the master " 'was angry, and delivered him to the torturers until he should pay all that was due to him' "—all that was already forgiven. And so, says Jesus, " 'My heavenly Father also will do to you if each of you, from his heart, does not forgive his brother his trespasses' " (Matthew 18:34, 35). Ellen White taught what Jesus taught.

The witness to Jesus

In his first letter, John wrote, "Beloved, do not believe every spirit, but test the spirits, whether they are of God; because many false prophets have gone out into the world. By this you know the Spirit of God: Every spirit that confesses that Jesus Christ has come in the flesh is of God" (1 John 4:1, 2). When John wrote these words, he was thinking of certain false teachers who denied that the Son of God had actually become a human being. They denied that "the Word became flesh" (John 1:14). In a broader sense, this test applies not only to the Incarnation but to everything the Bible teaches about Christ— His sinless life, His atoning death, His resurrection and ascension, His high priestly ministry in heaven, and His second coming. A true prophet will recognize and teach all these things.

Anyone familiar with the writings of Ellen White will have to admit that she not only accepted all that the Bible teaches about Jesus, but that she also continually pointed people to Him as their Lord and Savior. For example, "Look, O look to Jesus and live!"(FE 179). "Go to Jesus, and ask Him to forgive you, and then believe that He does" (HP 124). "It is our privilege to go to Jesus and be cleansed, and to stand before the law without shame or remorse" (SC 51).

Repeatedly she expressed her love for Jesus: "I love my Lord and Saviour, and it is my life to honor and glorify him upon the earth" (RH, April 19, 1870). "I love my Saviour this morning because He first loved me. If there is anything in my life, my words, my teachings that is good, it is because Christ has put it there. It is not because of any goodness in me, and there is no glory to be directed to myself" (11MR 241).

Fulfilled prophecy

The proof of a true prophet lies, in part, in the fulfillment of his or her predictions (see 1 Samuel 9:6; Jeremiah 28:9; Lamentations 3:37). Although Ellen White's work didn't primarily consist of predicting the future, she did make a number of predictions that have been fulfilled in a remarkable way. For example, on March 24, 1849, Ellen White wrote about the mysterious knocking that began in 1848 in the home of the Fox sisters at Hydesville, New York: "I saw that the mysterious knocking in New York and other places was the power of Satan, and that such things would be more and more common, clothed in a religious garb so as to lull the deceived to greater security" (EW 43). A year later she wrote, "I was shown that by the rapping and mesmerism these modern magicians would yet account for all the miracles wrought by our Lord Jesus Christ" (EW 59).

One hundred years later, in 1948, the *Centennial Book of Modern Spiritualism in America* was published. It claims that "spiritualism, with its signs, wonders, visions, and healing gifts was the religion of the Apostles; of the post-apostolic fathers, and the primitive Christians." Furthermore, it says, "A medium foretold the birth of Jesus, whose brief life on earth was filled with the performance of many so-called miracles which in reality were spiritual phenomena."[4]

Critics at times claim that Ellen White was a false prophet because some of her predictions have not come to pass. For example, concerning a conference in 1856, Mrs. White declared, "I was shown the company present at the Conference. Said the angel: 'Some food for worms, . . . some subjects of the seven last plagues, some will be alive and remain upon the earth to be translated at the coming of Jesus' " (1T 131). All who were alive then have long since died; thus this prediction was not fulfilled.

However, before we accuse Ellen White of being a false prophet, we should remember Jonah. What was the message God gave to Jonah for the Ninevites? " 'Yet forty days, and Nineveh shall be overthrown!' " (Jonah 3:4). Was Nineveh destroyed? No. Why not? Because the Ninevites changed their ways. The principle behind this story is the principle of conditional prophecy outlined in Jeremiah 18:7-10.

In the 1856 vision, God indicated to Ellen White that He wanted to bring in His kingdom within a short time, but events here on earth have delayed it. Therefore, in 1896 she wrote, "If those who claimed to have a living experience in the things of God had done their appointed work as the Lord ordained, the whole world would have been warned ere this, and the Lord Jesus would have come in power and great glory" (RH, Oct. 6, 1896). And in the last volume of the *Testimonies,* published in 1909, she wrote, "If every soldier of Christ had done his duty, if every watchman on the walls of Zion had given the trumpet a certain sound, the world might ere this have heard the message of warning. But the work is years behind. While men have slept, Satan has stolen a march upon us" (9T 29).

Ellen White clearly understood the principle of conditional prophecy, "The angels of God in their messages to men represent time as very short. Thus it has always been presented to me. It is true that time has continued longer than we expected in the early days of this message. Our Saviour did not appear as soon as we hoped. But has the Word of the Lord failed? Never! It should be remembered that the promises and the threatenings of God are alike conditional" (Ev 695). If we apply the principle of conditionality to her 1856 vision, the problem disappears.

The orchard test

The orchard test in Matthew 7:20, " 'by their fruits you will know them,' " requires time. Ellen White lived and worked for seventy years under the critical eyes of thousands of people who for the most part were skeptical, doubtful, suspicious, and in some cases openly hostile. Errors, faults, and inconsistencies were and still are exposed with great satisfaction by her opponents, but the fruit of her life and labor attest to her sincerity, zeal, and Christian piety. The lasting fruits of her labor will be discussed in more detail in chapter 12.

Francis M. Wilcox (1865–1951)

F. M. Wilcox, editor of the *Review and Herald* and an associate of Ellen White, wrote, "Her life and Christian experience conformed to the pure, simple, dignified principles of the gospel of Christ. She exemplified in her own life, as does every true prophet, the principles of truth she taught to others."[5] At the General Conference Session on June 7, 1946, he told the session participants, "The work of Mrs. White should not be judged by some detail, by the turn of a phrase or sentence, or by some seeming contradiction in her writings. It should be judged by the spirit which characterized her work through the years, by the fruit it has borne in connection with the great religious movement with which it was associated, and in the development of which it bore a prominent part and exerted a molding influence."[6]

Some people have difficulty accepting Ellen White's prophetic ministry because they stumble over certain details of her writings. They fail to see the bigger picture: the way God used her to raise up this church; the many wonderful insights she received from God; and the contributions she has made to this church. Like the Seventh-day Adventist Church, the Advent Christian Church had its origin in the Millerite movement. Its current membership stands at about thirty thousand. Apart from some doctrinal issues, the major difference between that church and the Adventist Church is the fact that God led the latter through the prophetic gift as manifested in the life and work of Ellen G. White. Without that gift, the Adventist Church would probably be a similar size to the Advent Christian Church—if it still existed at all.

Are there difficulties in the writings of Ellen White? Yes, but Scripture contains only a small portion of the writings of the biblical prophets, and still we find problems there. In the case of Ellen White, we have pretty much everything she wrote, so we shouldn't be surprised that there are "some things hard to understand," as Peter said of Paul's writings (2 Peter 3:16). In the cases of both Scripture and Ellen White's writings, we must focus on what is clear and profitable and suspend judgment on matters that seem ambiguous or contradictory.

CHAPTER 7

The Work of the Prophets

The life of a prophet was never an easy one. Isaiah was murdered, Jeremiah was put in prison, Daniel thrown to the lions, and Paul endured hardships a lesser mortal wouldn't have survived. "From the Jews five times I received forty stripes minus one. Three times I was beaten with rods; once I was stoned; three times I was shipwrecked; a night and a day I have been in the deep" (2 Corinthians 11:24, 25).

Although Ellen White was not, like Paul, physically assaulted by human beings, on more than one occasion Satan attempted to take her life. In 1858, while Ellen and her husband, James, were returning to Battle Creek after she received the great controversy vision in Lovett's Grove, Ohio, they stopped in Jackson, Michigan, to visit the Palmer family. The attack came while she was conversing with Mrs. Palmer. Describing what happened, she later wrote, "my tongue refused to utter what I wished to say, and seemed large and numb. A strange, cold sensation struck my heart, passed over my head, and down my right side. For a time I was insensible, but was aroused by the voice of earnest prayer" (LS 162).

Three months later, in a vision given to her in Battle Creek, she was shown who was really behind the distressing experience she suffered in the Palmer home. "In that vision I was shown that in the sudden attack at Jackson, Satan designed to take my life to hinder the work I was about to write; but angels of God were sent to my rescue, to raise me above the effects of Satan's attack. I saw, among other things, that I should be blest with better health than before the attack at Jackson" (3SM 100).

Besides the illnesses that plagued her from time to time, her life was far from easy. In the early years of her prophetic ministry, she and James were very poor and had to depend on others for living quarters and furniture. Since there was no paid ministry at that time, James worked hard hauling stones for the railroad and chopping wood for fifty cents a day to support his family and further the cause.

Two of the Whites' four children died young, and James wore himself out with travel, preaching, writing, and guiding the fledgling church from its beginning until 1881, when he died at the age of sixty. For the remaining thirty-four years of her life, Ellen White continued to labor, without her husband's support, as God's messenger to the remnant church. In the rest of this chapter, we will look at some of the functions she carried out in fulfilling her work as God's messenger.

Preaching the gospel

The gospel, or good news, is the central message of the New Testament. That "man is justified by faith apart from the deeds of the law" (Romans 3:28) was also the central message of the Reformers, such as Martin Luther and Ulrich Zwingli. Ellen White had a tremendous admiration for Martin Luther. The light of the Reformation was for her "the great doctrine of justification by faith, so clearly taught by Luther" (GC 253).

She accepted the gospel as presented by the Reformers and went even so far as to say, "Christ was a protestant. . . . The Reformers date back to Christ and the apostles. They came out and separated themselves from a religion of forms and ceremonies. Luther and his followers did not invent the reformed religion. They simply accepted it as presented by Christ and the apostles" (RH, June 1, 1886).

Ellen White recognized the need of preaching this gospel to our own members. "Our churches" she wrote, "are dying for the want of teaching on the subject of righteousness by faith in Christ, and for kindred truths" (RH, March 25, 1890).

In her proclamation of the gospel, she clearly distinguished the law from the gospel. The law presents the condition of eternal life, and that condition "is now just what it always has been,—just what it was in Paradise before the fall of our first parents,—perfect obedience to the law of God, perfect righteousness" (SC 62). The gospel supplies what the law demands. It directs us to Jesus, who is the perfect righteousness that the law demands. "Every soul may say: 'By His perfect obedience He has satisfied the claims of the law, and my only hope is found in looking to Him as my substitute and surety, who obeyed the law perfectly for me' " (1SM 396).

While Ellen White made a basic distinction between law and gospel, the emphasis in her writings was on the harmony of law and gospel. "We must present the law and the gospel together, for they go hand in hand" (GW 161). Repeatedly she admonished ministers to present both together, because "the law and the gospel, blended, will convict of sin. God's law, while condemning sin, points to the gospel, revealing Jesus Christ, in whom 'dwelleth all the fullness of the Godhead bodily.' . . . Thus both the law and the gospel are blended. In no discourse are they to be divorced" (Ev 231).

Ellen White also wrote much about sanctification, which she viewed as "the result of lifelong obedience" (AA 560). It is a process of divine grace that restores "in man the moral image of God" (MM 234). It is not the work of a moment, but "a refining process going on day by day, in God's own way, in doing His will until all true believers are complete in Him" (4MR 354). In proclaiming the gospel, Ellen White conformed very closely to the Protestant tradition.

Guiding God's people

In Hosea 12:13 we are told that "By a prophet the LORD brought Israel out of Egypt, / And by a prophet he was preserved." Preserving or protecting and guiding God's people was one of the main functions of the biblical prophets as well as of Ellen White's prophetic ministry. Apart from writing the many books published during her lifetime,* for more than thirty-five years Ellen White contributed important articles almost every week to the periodicals published by the church in English, German, Danish-Norwegian, and other languages. Church members came to look for these weekly articles as messages from the Lord. Frequently they were used in the Sabbath meetings when no minister was present.

In these articles, Ellen White dealt with a variety of topics of theological and practical significance. One topic that she addressed repeatedly was the

---

* When Ellen White died in 1915, twenty-four of her books were in circulation and two were almost ready for the printer.

home[1]—the joy and love and peace that should be found in a Christian home. Another topic she dealt with frequently was health[2]—lessons on health, and encouragement to faithfulness in health reform. "The gospel is to be bound up with the principles of true health reform," she counseled (6T 379).

From time to time, she gave practical counsel on Christian living. How to keep the Sabbath was an important topic. "All needful preparation for the Sabbath should be made on Friday," she said. "On Sabbath morning, if the weather is cool, let hot gruel be provided. Further than this, all cooking should be avoided as a violation of the Sabbath" (RH, May 8, 1883).

In these weekly articles, she touched on a variety of topics. In reply to the question "Should Christians dance?" she wrote that "dancing has no place in the Christian's life. When you feel a desire to engage in this amusement, go in imagination to Gethsemane, and behold the anguish which Christ endured for us" (RH, Feb. 28, 1882). On the topic of jewelry she stated, "To dress plainly, abstaining from display of jewelry and ornaments of every kind, is in keeping with our faith" (3T 366). And on the duty of forgiveness she advised, "We must imitate the long-suffering of God toward us" (RH, Nov. 16, 1886). Some of the other topics with which she dealt were "Exacting Usury of Brethren" (RH, March 11, 1884), "May Christians Manufacture Wine and Cider?" (RH, March 25, 1884), "Unwise Marriages" (RH, Feb. 2, 1886), and "How to Deal With the Erring" (RH, Nov. 25, 1902).

While Ellen White was alive, these weekly messages guided the leadership of the church—when they were willing to listen. The messages "exercised a most helpful influence in uniting, organizing, inspiring, and keeping the advent movement. Even ministers of other churches made use of them."[3]

Meeting fanaticism

From the very beginning of her ministry, Ellen G. White had to meet fanaticism and opposition. Some people claimed to be perfect; others that no more work should be done; and some kept on setting times for Christ's return.

Once, during a time when a group of fanatics in the vicinity of Boston strongly opposed Ellen White's ministry, she was taken off in vision for more than four hours. In 1859, Otis Nichols described what took place on that occasion:

Sargent, Robbins, and French [leaders among these fanatics]

were much exasperated as well as excited to hear Sister White talk in vision, which they declared was of the devil. They exhausted all their influence and bodily strength to destroy the effect of the vision. They would unite in singing very loud, and then alternately would talk and read from the Bible in a loud voice in order that Ellen might not be heard, until their strength was exhausted and their hands would shake, so they could not read from the Bible.

But amidst all this confusion and noise, Ellen's clear and shrill voice as she talked in vision was distinctly heard by all present.[4]

Otis Nichols (1798–1876)

Mr. Thayer, the owner of the house, had heard that one could arrest visions produced by satanic power by opening the Bible and laying it on the visionary person. He took a heavy family Bible and laid it open upon Mrs. White's chest. While still in vision, she took the Bible and lifted it up as high as she could reach. Holding the Bible in one hand and turning the pages with the other without looking at them, she pointed to a number of Bible passages and, still without looking at them, quoted them correctly. Nichols recalled "Some of the passages referred to were judgments against the wicked and blasphemous; and others were admonitions and instructions relative to our present condition.

"In this state she continued all the afternoon until nearly sundown when she came out of vision."[5]

As a result, the fanatics were silenced, and those who had been unsure were convinced that God was indeed leading the little band of Advent believers through the gift of prophecy.

Reproving sin

The entrance of sin into this world through the fall of our first parents led the whole human race into sin (Romans 5:12; 3:23). To remedy the situation, Christ came and died on the cross (John 3:16; Romans 5:10). Before He returned to heaven, He promised to send the Comforter, the

Holy Spirit. "When he is come," Christ said, "he will reprove the world of sin, and of righteousness, and of judgment" (John 16:8, KJV).

No one enjoys being reproved for sins committed, yet prophets, as well as ministers today, are called upon to reprove sin in the church. Ellen White said this was one of the most difficult assignments she received. To reprove private sins was for her a most "disagreeable work" (LS 177). However, "I was shown," she wrote, "that God has laid this work upon us" (3T 259). Yet, she knew that "some will not listen to caution or reproof" (RH Supplement, 1881).

Stephen Smith

The sad result of this kind of attitude is seen in the story of Stephen Smith and an unread testimony.[6] In 1850, Smith and his wife accepted the Adventist message. Smith loved the Sabbath, but he was prone to being led astray by people who claimed to have new light, and he was opposed to Ellen White and her visions. So he left the church.

Mrs. White received a vision that revealed what Smith's life would be like if he persisted in the course he was following. She wrote out a letter telling what she had seen and appealing to him to turn from his waywardness. When Smith received the letter, he feared that it was a testimony of reproof, so without opening it, he tucked it deep in a trunk. For twenty-eight years that testimony lay at the bottom of the trunk, unopened and unread.

Although Smith had left the church, his wife remained faithful. She continued to receive the *Review and Herald,* and one day, twenty-seven years after Smith had turned from the church, he picked up a copy of that magazine and read an article Ellen White had written. Finding that her article spoke to his heart, he continued to read her articles each week, and he began to soften.

During the following year (1885), Elder Eugene Farnsworth held revival meetings in Washington, New Hampshire, not too far from the Smith home. Smith had known Eugene as a lad and had seen him grow up, so he decided to attend the meetings. Upon hearing Farnsworth's messages, he gave his heart to the Lord again. Then he remembered the letter

Ellen White had written to him twenty-eight years before. He pulled it out of the trunk, opened it, and in it read a description of his life during the past twenty-eight years—with all the bitterness and disappointments he had experienced.

The next Sabbath Smith told his story to the church members gathered to worship. He said, " 'I received a testimony myself twenty-eight years ago. I took it home and locked it up in my trunk, and I never read it till last Thursday. . . . Every word of the testimony for me is true, and I accept it. And I have come to that place where I finally believe they [Ellen White's testimonies] all are of God, and if I had heeded the one God sent to me as well as the rest, it would have changed the whole course of my life, and I should have been a very different man.' "[7]

How much better this man's life could have been if he had listened to the counsel and admonition of the Lord's servant! Reproving sin is a mark of a true prophet—something God inspires the prophet to do for our benefit.

Predicting the future

With few exceptions, predicting the future was only a small part of the work of biblical prophets. We find the same to be true of the life and work of Ellen White; her work consisted primarily in counseling and guiding the church. However, she was given a number of prophecies, particularly in regard to end-time events.

One of the most interesting of her prophecies is found in *Testimonies,* volume 5. In 1885 she wrote, "When Protestantism shall stretch her hand across the gulf to grasp the hand of the Roman power, when she shall reach over the abyss to clasp hands with spiritualism, when under the influence of this threefold union, our country shall repudiate every principle of its Constitution as a Protestant and republican government, and shall make provision for the propagation of papal falsehoods and delusions, then we may know that the time has come for the marvelous working of Satan and that the end is near" (5T 451).

In 1885 the ecumenical movement as we know it today was a long way off in the future. At that time, not only were Protestants quarreling among themselves in regard to "sheep stealing" in the mission fields, but most of them were violently opposed to the Roman Catholic Church as well—as some still are today in Northern Ireland.

The idea of an ecumenical movement was conceived at the 1910 World Missionary Conference in Edinburgh. However, because of the First and Second World Wars, almost another forty years passed before the ecumenical baby was born. In 1948, 351 delegates from 147 Protestant churches gathered in Amsterdam, Holland, to organize the World Council of Churches. Since then, the ecumenical movement has grown. Today, about 340 churches with almost 600 million members belong to the World Council of Churches, which is headquartered in Geneva, Switzerland.

During the first twelve years after 1948, only Protestant churches belonged to the World Council of Churches. Then in 1961, the Orthodox churches began to join, and by 1964, practically all the Orthodox churches were members of that organization. However, the largest Christian church—the Roman Catholic Church, with more than one billion members—still has not joined the World Council of Churches as a member. What then about Ellen White's prediction that "Protestantism shall stretch her hand across the gulf to grasp the hand of the Roman power"?

On March 29, 1994, forty leading evangelical Protestants and Roman Catholics—people such as Pat Robertson and John Cardinal O'Connor—signed a document titled "Evangelicals and Catholics Together: The Christian Mission in the Third Millennium."[8] Headlines emblazoned upon newspapers across America stated, "Christians Herald New Era" and "Catholics Embrace Evangelicals—Conservatives of Both Faiths Agreed to Accept Each Other as Christians."

In 1995 a book appeared with the title: *Evangelicals and Catholics Together: Toward a Common Mission.* In it the authors claim that "European Catholics and Protestants [have] . . . concluded that the condemnations of the Reformation were based on misconceptions, were aimed at extreme positions on the other side, and no longer apply to today's situations."[9] One wonders what Martin Luther and the thousands who gave their lives for the principles of the Reformation would say to that. But Ellen White's prediction, which must have seemed far-fetched at the time, should have led us to expect just such a development.

CHAPTER

The Authority of the Prophets

In 1902 Dr. Daniel Kress became the first medical director of the newly built Sydney Adventist Hospital. He was a very careful health reformer who took Ellen White's counsel seriously. When he read in the *Testimonies* that Ellen White had written to a family, "Eggs should not be placed upon your table" (2T 400),* he deleted eggs from his diet. By giving up not only eggs but also milk, butter, and cheese, he brought upon himself a very serious case of anemia. His prospects for living became rather uncertain.

Daniel H. Kress (1862–1956)   Mrs. White, who was in California, was given a vision that revealed Dr. Kress's condition. She was also shown that he should return to the use of dairy products and that he should use raw egg in grape juice every day, for it would save his life (12MR 169). Dr. Kress,

* Some have given a general application to the admonition in the personal testimony addressed to brother and sister E that "Eggs should not be placed upon your table." That this was not intended as a general teaching for families in normal circumstances is made clear not only by the setting of the statement itself but also by no less than three specific published utterances of Ellen G. White that would correct any misapplication of this personal testimony. These are found in 7T 135 (1902), MH 320 (1905), and 9T 162 (1909).

The Gift of Prophecy

who accepted Ellen White's prophetic authority, followed her counsel. He turned from his extreme interpretation of health reform, regained his health, and served the cause of God for nearly fifty years after that.

What authority should the writings of Ellen G. White have in our lives?

Prophetic authority

The Bible reveals clearly that God is the true source and center of authority (see Genesis 17:1; Psalm 83:18). As Creator and Lord of all nature and history, He has the right to exercise authority over humankind (see Psalm 96:2-6; Isaiah 45:22, 23).

In Old Testament times, God appointed certain people to serve as His prophets (see 1 Samuel 3:30; 9:9; 2 Samuel 7:2). He communicated with them through visions and dreams (see Numbers 12:6). They were God's authoritative spokespersons to His people, just as Aaron was the authorized spokesperson for Moses (see Jeremiah 13:12; Ezekiel 24:21; Exodus 4:16). In the time of the New Testament, Jesus authorized His disciples and the New Testament prophets to proclaim His message. So Paul could say, "You received the Word of God which you heard from us . . . not as the word of men, but as it is in truth, the Word of God" (1 Thessalonians 2:13).

The prophetic word has authority because God gives it His authority. Moses knew that he was authorized to speak on God's behalf. Isaiah knew it. Paul and Peter knew it (see, for instance, 2 Corinthians 10:8). And the people of God accepted them as God's messengers.

In the Bible we find canonical prophets such as Moses and Jeremiah—prophets whose writings became part of the biblical canon, the books that make up the Bible. Scripture also tells us about prophets such as Nathan (see 1 Chronicles 29:29), Ahijah, and Iddo (see 2 Chronicles 9:29)—prophets whose books, though inspired, didn't become part of the biblical canon. (They're called "noncanonical prophets.") We don't know why God selected some books by inspired prophets to be in the Bible and left out others that equally inspired prophets had written. Obviously, He knew what humankind would need to understand the plan of salvation.

What the noncanonical prophets said or wrote was just as authoritative for the people of their time as were the books of Moses and Isaiah. For example, after David's sin with Bathsheba, the prophet Nathan brought him a message from God. Now, the Bible of David's time was the Torah—the first five books of the Old Testament. Nathan hadn't written anything that was in the Bible. But not for one moment did David question Nathan's authority. He knew that Nathan was a prophet and that Nathan's word was authoritative for him (see 2 Samuel 12:7-14). The authority of a prophet is based on his or her inspiration; and the authority of the prophet's writings is based on their inspiration, not on their place in the canon.

Since the time of John the revelator, the biblical canon has been closed, and no other inspired books can be added to it. If archaeologists were to find the book of Nathan today, it wouldn't be added to the canon but would remain an inspired book outside of the canon. And whatever theological statements it contained would remain inspired and authoritative statements, though they were outside the canon. The canon is simply the collection of books that was put together under God's guidance as the rule of faith and practice for God's people. The canon is the standard by which everything else has to be measured. It contains everything a person needs to know to be saved.

The apostle Paul wrote a number of inspired letters that were lost—for example, his letter to the Laodiceans (see Colossians 4:16) and the letter he wrote to the Corinthians before he wrote what we know as 1 Corinthians (see 1 Corinthians 5:9). If someone found these letters today, they wouldn't become part of the Bible but would remain inspired letters outside of the canon.

The writings of Ellen White

Scripture is God's message for all time and all people. It is the measuring rod, the yardstick against which everything else has to be measured—the supreme guide for every Christian. The writings of Ellen White, on the other hand, are God's messages for a particular people, His remnant church, at a particular time in history, the end time. Her writings aren't a new or additional standard of doctrine but a help for the church in the time of the end. Hence her writings have a different purpose from that of Scripture. They are the "lesser light to lead men and women to the greater light" (CM 125).

In 1982 *Ministry* magazine published the following statement of affirmations and denials issued by the Biblical Research Institute in regard to the Ellen G. White writings.[1] Although it never became an officially voted statement of the church, it is a good summary of the relationship between the writings of Ellen G. White and the Bible.

The Gift of Prophecy

Affirmations

1. We believe that Scripture is the divinely revealed Word of God and is inspired by the Holy Spirit.

2. We believe that the canon of Scripture is composed only of the sixty-six books of the Old and New Testaments.

3. We believe that Scripture is the foundation of faith and the final authority in all matters of doctrine and practice.

4. We believe that Scripture is the Word of God in human language.

5. We believe that Scripture teaches that the gift of prophecy will be manifest in the Christian church after New Testament times.

6. We believe that the ministry and writings of Ellen White were a manifestation of the gift of prophecy.

7. We believe that Ellen White was inspired by the Holy Spirit and that her writings, the product of that inspiration, are particularly applicable and authoritative to Seventh-day Adventists.

8. We believe that the purposes of the Ellen White writings include guidance in understanding the teaching of Scripture and application of these teachings with prophetic urgency to the spiritual and moral life.

9. We believe that the acceptance of the prophetic gift of Ellen White, while not a requirement for continuing church membership, is important to the nurture and unity of the Seventh-day Adventist Church.

10. We believe that Ellen White's use of literary sources and assistants finds parallels in some of the writings of the Bible.

Denials

1. We do not believe that the quality or degree of inspiration in the writings of Ellen White is different from that of Scripture.

2. We do not believe that the writings of Ellen White serve the same purpose as does Scripture, which is the sole foundation and final authority of Christian faith.

3. We do not believe that the writings of Ellen White are an addition to the canon of sacred Scripture.

4. We do not believe that the writings of Ellen White may be used as the basis of doctrine.

5. We do not believe that the study of the writings of Ellen White may be used to replace the study of Scripture.

6. We do not believe that Scripture can be understood only through the

writings of Ellen White.

7. We do not believe that the writings of Ellen White exhaust the meaning of Scripture.

8. We do not believe that the writings of Ellen White are essential for the proclamation of the truths of Scripture to society at large.

9. We do not believe that the inspired writings of Ellen White are merely the product of Christian piety.

10. We do not believe that Ellen White's use of literary sources and assistants negates the inspiration of her writings.

These affirmations and denials clearly indicate that while as a church, Seventh-day Adventists say the quality or degree of inspiration in the writings of Ellen White is no different from that of Scripture, to quote the denial: "We do not believe that the writings of Ellen White are an addition to the canon of Sacred Scripture." It was concluded, therefore, that "a correct understanding of the inspiration and authority of the writings of Ellen White will avoid two extremes: (1) regarding these writings as functioning on a canonical level identical with Scripture, or (2) considering them as ordinary Christian literature."[2]

The authority of the Ellen G. White writings

Seventh-day Adventists reject the idea that there are degrees of inspiration. They believe that Ellen White was a messenger of God and that she was inspired like the Old and New Testament prophets. The question, then, is, If Ellen White was as inspired as the Old and New Testament prophets, what authority do her writings have?

Since Mrs. White's writings are not an addition to the Bible, her books fall into the same category as the writings of the noncanonical prophets. Her writings, therefore, have the same authority that the writings of the noncanonical prophets had for their time.

Ellen White left her readers in no doubt about the source of her writings. There are only two possibilities: " 'God is either teaching His church, reproving their wrongs and strengthening their faith, or He is not. This work is of God, or it is not. God does nothing in partnership with Satan. My work . . . bears the stamp of God or the stamp of the enemy. There is no halfway work in the matter. The *Testimonies* are of the Spirit of God, or of the devil' " (5T 671). In a letter to the church in Battle Creek, she wrote,

" 'I do not write one article in the paper, expressing merely my own ideas. They are what God has opened before me in vision—the precious rays of light shining from the throne' " (1SM 27).

Because the source of what she wrote was divine, her words have authority. To those who refused to accept her writings as having divine authority she said, " 'when I send you a testimony of warning and reproof, many of you declare it to be merely the opinion of Sister White. You have thereby insulted the Spirit of God. You know how the Lord has manifested Himself through the Spirit of prophecy [a metonym for the writings of Ellen White]' " (1SM 27).

At the same time, she emphasized her submission to the Bible, which she called "the greater light" (CM 125). "We are to receive God's word as supreme authority" (6T 402), she wrote, and "the Holy Scriptures are to be accepted as an authoritative, infallible revelation of His will. They are the standard of character, the revealer of doctrines, and the test of experience" (GC vii). Therefore, she said, "the testimonies of Sister White should not be carried to the front. God's Word is the unerring standard. . . . Let all prove their positions from the Scriptures and substantiate every point they claim as truth from the revealed Word of God" (Ev 256). At a meeting held in the Battle Creek College library on the eve of the General Conference of 1901, she told the leaders, "Lay Sister White to one side. Do not quote my words again as long as you live until you can obey the Bible" (13MR 248).

Yet she didn't consider these admonitions to have denied the manifestation of the prophetic gift in her ministry. "The fact that God has revealed His will to men through His word, has not rendered needless the continued presence and guiding of the Holy Spirit. On the contrary, the Spirit was promised by our Saviour, to open the word to His servants, to illuminate and apply its teachings" (GC vii).

Some Adventists believe that her authority is only pastoral—faith-strengthening but not faith-building. In other words, they believe that she has no teaching or dogmatic authority. This differentiation between the pastoral and the teaching authority of a prophet, however, is not scriptural. The Bible makes no distinction between a prophet's pastoral and his or her teaching functions. Prophets are God's spokespersons whatever the content of the message. "Any claim that Ellen White's writings carry no teaching authority must fly in the face of her own statements. As we have seen, she declares unequivocally, 'My commission embraces that of a prophet, but it does not end there.' She either told the truth or she didn't. If she didn't, what further confidence could we have in her even if she honestly but mistakenly thought so?"[3]

Above all, we shouldn't forget what the main theme of all her writings was. The first sentence in her book *Patriarch and Prophets* says "God is love," and the last sentence in her book *The Great Controversy* also reads "God is love." And between these first and the last pages of the whole Conflict of the Ages Series, she revealed God's love for humanity. Her main theme was always Jesus. Constantly she pointed people to Scripture and Jesus Christ. Her whole life was devoted to making Jesus the center of our faith.

In 1980 a survey was taken among Seventh-day Adventists. Of those who regularly read Ellen White's writings, 85 percent stated that they had a close personal relationship with Christ. Only 59 percent of those who didn't read her regularly said the same. Those who said they regularly read her books also stated that they study Scripture daily. Of those who didn't read her works, only 47 percent said they read Scripture regularly.[4] Furthermore, in most churches, it's frequently the avid readers of her books who are the missionary-minded people.

If the reading of Mrs. White's books makes people read more in Scripture and makes them more missionary minded, should we not encourage all Seventh-day Adventists to read her books?

Ellen White as a theologian

While Ellen White had no theological training, through divine inspiration she received theological insights that not only saved the Advent movement from many a heresy in its early years, but that have stood the test of time.

On the basis of divine revelations throughout her ministry, Ellen White was able to guide the church not only in a pastoral way but from time to time also in matters of theology. In 1898, for example, she spoke out strongly against the view of Uriah Smith and others that Jesus hadn't existed as a separate being forever but had a beginning (see DA 530). In 1901, she put an end to the "holy flesh" teaching in Indiana (she called it a "satanic deception" [2SM 31]). And from 1903 on, she drew the line on Kellogg's pantheism, which she termed "the alpha of deadly heresies" (1SM 200).

At the same time we must remember that when she had no light on a particular matter she was silent. When some of the denomination's leaders pressured her to settle the question of the "daily," she told them, "I have had no instruction on the point under discussion" (1SM 164). Similarly, she was silent in regard to such matters as the "eastern question" or who would constitute the 144,000 because she had no light from God on these issues.

While Ellen White was open to new light and new interpretations of Scripture (CW 35), she insisted that any new light had to harmonize with the distinctive truths of the church that had been established under divine guidance. "We are not to receive the words of those who come with a message that contradicts the special points of our faith" (1SM 161).

Is her theology still valid today? Yes! However, we need to remember that in the interpretation of Scripture, her writings are generally homiletical or evangelistic in nature and not exegetical. Thus, her writings should not be used to settle issues of textual interpretation until it has been established how she used a biblical text (see chapter 11).

The pioneers of the Seventh-day Adventist Church recognized the tremendous value and the authority of the writings of Ellen White. While they upheld the Scriptures as the "only rule of faith and practice," they accepted the prophetic gift of Ellen White as God-given. In 1847, James White wrote in regard to the relationship between Scripture and the visions of Ellen White: "The bible [sic] is a perfect and complete revelation. It is our only rule of faith and practice. But this is no reason, why God may not show the past, present, and future fulfillment of his word, in these *last days,* by dreams and visions; according to Peter's testimony. True visions are given to lead us to God, and his written word; but those that are given for a new rule of faith and practice, separate from the bible, cannot be from God, and should be rejected."[5]

In 1855, the leadership of the Advent movement publicly stated that they regarded the writings of Ellen White as coming from God. Therefore, "we must acknowledge ourselves under obligation to abide by their teachings, and be corrected by their admonitions."[6] Ever since then, General Conferences in session have from time to time issued statements expressing confidence in the writings of Ellen White "as the teaching of the Spirit of God,"[7] though subordinate to the Bible, which is God's measuring rod, or standard, for all time and all people.

Fundamental Belief number 18 clearly states that Ellen G. White's "writings are a continuing and authoritative source of truth which provide for the church comfort, guidance, instruction, and correction."[8] Though nearly a century has elapsed since Ellen White laid down her pen, her inspired and therefore authoritative writings continue to be a guiding and unifying factor in the Seventh-day Adventist Church.

The Integrity of the Prophetic Gift

According to the dictionary, integrity is "rigid adherence to a code of behavior" or "the state of being unimpaired; soundness." Synonyms of the word *integrity* are *uprightness* and *honesty*.

Bible-believing Christians hardly ever question the integrity of the biblical prophets, but what about the integrity of modern prophets—specifically, the integrity of Ellen White? Critics inside and outside of the church have written articles and books disputing her prophetic ministry and casting doubt on her integrity. Some of these challenges have been answered in other places in this book. In this chapter, we will touch on two commonly cited criticisms of her writings—the "shut-door" question and the issue of plagiarism.

William Miller (1782–1849)

The "shut-door" question

The shut-door concept originated with William Miller. He first articulated his understanding in 1836, in a lecture on the parable of the ten virgins. In that parable, when the five foolish virgins return from buying oil for their lamps, they find that the door to the wedding "was shut"

(Matthew 25:10). Just prior to October 1844, Miller believed that the door of mercy for the world had been closed, and he continued to believe, until early in 1845, that the work of warning sinners was finished and that their time of probation had ended.[1]

Like other Millerite Adventists, Ellen White accepted Miller's view of the shut door and believed for a time after the Great Disappointment in 1844 that the door of mercy for sinners was shut. In 1874 she wrote, "With my brethren and sisters, after the time passed in forty-four I did believe no more sinners would be converted. But I never had a vision that no more sinners would be converted. And am clear and free to state no one has ever heard me say or has read from my pen statements which will justify them in the charges they have made against me upon this point" (1SM 74).

In Ellen White's first vision (December 1844), she saw the Advent people traveling on a straight and narrow path to the heavenly Jerusalem. "They had a bright light set up behind them at the first end of the path, which an angel told me was the Midnight Cry. This light shone all along the path, and gave light for their feet so they might not stumble. And if they kept their eyes fixed on Jesus, who was just before them, leading them to the City, they were safe."[2]

Some, however, took their eyes off Jesus and denied that God had led them thus far. They fell off the path down into "the dark and wicked world below. It was just as impossible for them to get on the path again and go to the City, as all the wicked world which God had rejected."[3] This is how she at first described what she had seen in the vision. Given her Millerite background, this description is understandable.

When the vision was reprinted in the book *Christian Experience and Teachings of Ellen G. White* in 1851, the last sentence in the above quote was left out. This led to the charge that she suppressed this statement because it taught that God had rejected the whole world. In 1883, she responded to these charges. She said,

> It is claimed that these expressions prove the shut-door doctrine, and that this is the reason of their omission in later editions. But in fact they teach only that which has been and is still held by us as a people, as I shall show.
>
> For a time after the disappointment in 1844, I did hold, in common with the advent body, that the door of mercy was then forever

closed to the world. This position was taken before my first vision was given me. It was the light given me of God that corrected our error, and enabled us to see the true position.

I am still a believer in the shut-door theory, but not in the sense in which we at first employed the term or in which it is employed by my opponents (1SM 62, 63).

Ellen White had received her second major vision in February 1845. In it she saw Jesus still ministering before the Father as our great High Priest (EW 55). In the fall of the same year, she had another vision in which she was shown that the time of trouble was still in the future.[4] Thus she could write in 1883, "Those who did not see the light, had not the guilt of its rejection. It was only the class who had despised the light from heaven that the Spirit of God could not reach. And this class included, as I have stated, both those who refused to accept the message when it was presented to them, and also those who, having received it, afterward renounced their faith" (1SM 63, 64).

Finally, her visions received in March and April 1847 clearly indicated that there was still an evangelistic work to be done. She saw Jesus by the ark of the covenant in the Most Holy Place. He had the tables of stone, which folded together like a book. Jesus opened them, and she saw that the four commandments on the first table shone brighter than the other six, and the fourth, the Sabbath commandment, shone brighter than all the rest. "I saw that God had children, who do not see and keep the Sabbath. They had not rejected the light on it. And at the commencement of the [little] time of trouble, we were filled with the Holy Ghost as we went forth [Hos. 6:2, 3] and proclaimed the Sabbath more fully."[5] Thus, by 1847, the view that probation was closed for sinners had largely disappeared.

It seems that Ellen White didn't fully understand, at first, what was shown to her in those early visions, not only because she was still a young girl in her late teens but also because she was steeped in the Millerite thinking that probation for sinners was closed. Later in life she freely admitted, "Often representations are given me which at first I do not understand, but after a time they are made plain by a repeated presentation of those things that I did not at first comprehend, and in ways that make their meaning clear and unmistakable" (3SM 56). This also happened in connection with her understanding of the shut door. She was led step by step to an understanding of what had happened on October 22, 1844. The Holy Spirit not only gave her the visions, He also guided her to a fuller comprehension of them.

On this issue Herbert Douglass wrote, "As she developed the meaning of the events seen in her first vision, and her mind became sensitive to the truths implicit in certain Biblical expositions of others, her theological insights not only completely changed the direction of her life but set the agenda for the Seventh-day Adventist movement."[6]

Plagiarism

The chapter in this book on the inspiration of the prophets showed that, like some of the biblical authors, Ellen White used passages from the writings of others to put on paper what God had shown her in vision or what the Holy Spirit led her to write. In 1980, Walter Rea, at that time a minister of the Seventh-day Adventist Church in Long Beach, California, gave an interview to the *Los Angeles Times*[7] in which he made three allegations: (1) Mrs. White was a thief—she stole the literary productions of others. (2) She was a liar—she denied that she did it. And (3) she and her husband exploited the church members and made a fortune from her books. Then in 1982, Rea published the book *The White Lie* in which he has about one hundred pages of two-column comparisons of statements from Ellen White's books that resemble what other authors had written previously.

Plagiarism is the taking of ideas and/or wording from another person's publications and passing them off as one's own. The officers of the General Conference considered Rea's allegations to be so serious that they asked the General Conference's legal office to have them investigated. The legal officers asked attorney Vincent L. Ramik, a Roman Catholic lawyer specializing in patent, trademark, and copyright law, to do the investigation.

Ramik read the book *The Great Controversy* all the way through and spent about three hundred hours reading in many of Ellen White's other books and researching about one thousand relevant cases in American legal history. He concluded that Ellen White was not a plagiarist and that her works do not constitute copyright infringements. In his report he stated,

> I believe that the critics have missed the boat badly by focusing upon Mrs. White's *writings*, instead of focusing upon the *messages* in Mrs. White's writings. . . .

The Integrity of the Prophetic Gift

Ellen White used the writings of others; but in the *way* she used them, she made them uniquely her own, ethically, as well as legally. And, interestingly, she invariably improved that which she "selected"! . . .

. . . Ellen White [used] . . . words, phrases, clauses, sentences, paragraphs, yes, and even pages, from the writings of those who went before her. She stayed well within the legal boundaries of "fair use," and all the time created something that was substantially greater (and even more beautiful) than the mere sum of the component parts. And I think the ultimate tragedy is that the critics fail to see this.[8]

Nineteenth-century standards

Ellen White's borrowing may have been legal, but was it ethical? Was it acceptable, common practice in her time? Why did she not always use quotation marks when using passages from other books? What do we know about the standards of writing in the nineteenth century?

In his *History in the United States, 1800–1860,* George H. Callcott said the following about the writing of nineteenth-century historians:

> Despite their emphasis on honest scholarship, the Romantic historians have suffered grievously at the hands of subsequent scholars, for they have been accused of dishonesty, of altering direct quotations, and of using each other's material without the scrupulous use of quotation marks. . . . However, accusations of dishonesty were unjust, for the historians were never secretive about their practices, and they must be judged by their own standards. It had never occurred to many that accurate quoting was desirable.[9]

A second major assault by modern critics on the historians of the early nineteenth century centers on the issue of plagiarism—"the practice of using in their own works the same phraseology as someone else had used. The early nineteenth-century historian would have been dismayed by the attack, would have pleaded *nolo contendere,* and would simply have pointed out that he had never pretended to be original when he could find someone else who had satisfactorily said what he had in mind."[10]

Furthermore, "The early nineteenth-century historian felt no need to argue for originality, and he would not have understood why he should make a fetish of reworking material when what he wanted to say already had been said better by another. . . .

"Historians usually felt flattered rather than insulted when their words were used by another."[11]

It is true that toward the end of the nineteenth century, plagiarism became more of an issue and people began to be more careful in using sources. When the book *The Great Controversy* was revised in 1910–11, Ellen White instructed her staff to give proper credit to the sources wherever that was possible. Nevertheless, during most of the nineteenth century, religious writers in particular felt that they could freely use whatever contributed to their objective of advancing the kingdom of God.

Ellen White read widely and had a retentive memory, which meant that she often used material she had read without going back to her library to find out exactly where it was found. Furthermore, God told her "that in the reading of religious books and journals, she would find precious gems of truth expressed in acceptable language, and that she would be given help from heaven to recognize these and to separate them from the rubbish of error with which she would sometimes find them associated."[12] So far from trying to hide her use of the writings of others, she explained in print how and why she did it.[13] She even recommended that people read the books she used in writing her own works.* Her work as an author was in accordance with the customs of her time. As we have seen, she broke no copyright laws. Her conduct was defensible both legally and morally.

During Ellen White's lifetime and ever since her death, critics have questioned her integrity. She has been accused of deception, falsehood, and lies. One major reason for these accusations has been presuppositions about how a prophet should function. For example, some critics believe that "prophets 'should have full knowledge' from the start of their ministry; their predictions should be unalterable, their writings exempt from all errors, discrepancies, and mistakes, and never include uninspired sources. For them, prophets never express merely personal opinions in their writings."[14]

---

* For example, she recommended in *Signs of the Times®*, Feb. 22, 1883, 96, the book *The Life and Epistles of St. Paul* by Conybeare and Howson, which she used in her book *Sketches From the Life of Paul*; and in the *Review and Herald*, Dec. 26, 1882, 789, she wrote, "For those who can procure it, D'Aubigne's *History of the Reformation* will be both interesting and profitable." She used D'Aubigne's books in writing *The Great Controversy*.

As we have seen in our study of biblical prophets, these presuppositions assume a verbal-inspiration concept that Seventh-day Adventists do not hold.

Ellen White's personal integrity was confirmed many times by those who worked with her as well as by those who were not Seventh-day Adventists. Upon her death, *The Independent,* a weekly journal published in New York, devoted a column to her life and work. It concluded with these words: " 'she was absolutely honest in her belief in her revelations. Her life was worthy of them. She showed no spiritual pride and she sought no filthy lucre. She lived the life and did the work of a worthy prophetess[,] the most admirable of the American succession.' "[15]

Responses to the major challenges to her writings can be found in the following books: F. D. Nichol, *Ellen G. White and Her Critics* (Washington, D.C.: Review and Herald®, 1951); Arthur L. White, *The Ellen G. White Writings* (Washington, D.C.: Review and Herald®, 1973); Robert Olson, *One Hundred and One Questions on the Sanctuary and on Ellen White* (Washington, D.C.: Ellen G. White Estate, 1981); Herbert E. Douglass, *Messenger of the Lord* (Nampa, Idaho: Pacific Press®, 1998); and Leonard Brand and Don S. McMahon, *The Prophet and Her Critics* (Nampa, Idaho: Pacific Press®, 2005).

The End-time Prophet and End-time Events

The doctrinal framework of the Seventh-day Adventist Church was largely adopted during a series of weekend gatherings that were generally known as "the Sabbath conferences." More than a dozen such conferences were held in the years 1848–1850. Ellen White, in describing the beliefs of the approximately thirty-five attendees, wrote that "hardly two agreed. Some were holding serious errors, and each strenuously urged his own views, declaring that they were according to the Scriptures" (LS 110). Yet, invariably, when the weekend was over, there was unity of belief. What happened to bring this unanimity out of such diversity?

First, there was earnest Bible study and prayer. Writing in 1904, more than a half century after the events, Ellen White still had vivid memories of the conferences. "Often we remained together until late at night, and sometimes through the entire night, praying for light and studying the Word" (1SM 206).

But Bible study and prayer alone weren't enough to convince the participants. In addition, the conferences saw the direct intervention of the Holy Spirit. However, this intervention didn't come until the participants had gone as far as they could go. "When they came to the point in their study where they said, 'We can do nothing more,' the Spirit of the Lord would come upon me, I would be taken off in vision, and a clear explanation of the passages we had been studying would be given me" (1SM 206).

The function of the visions given at the conferences appears to have been to correct those Bible students when they were on the wrong track and to confirm and corroborate when they were on the right track, but never to initiate doctrinal formulation. The visions weren't given to take the place of faith, initiative, hard work, and Bible study. God didn't use the Spirit of prophecy to make the people dependent on the visions.

The writings of Ellen White touch on many different topics. One issue to which she returned repeatedly was eschatology—the doctrine of events at the end of time.

Ellen White's teaching about the end time was built on the historicist method of prophetic interpretation. That is, she understood the four world empires in Daniel 2 and 7 as being Babylon, Media-Persia, Greece, and Rome (Ed 177); the 1,260 "years" of Daniel 7:25 as pointing to the period of papal supremacy from 538 to 1798 (GC 266); the deadly wound mentioned in Revelation 13:3 as referring to Napoleon I's taking Pope Pius VI prisoner (GC 266); the 2,300 years of Daniel 8:14 as beginning in 457 B.C. and ending in 1844 (GC 328); and that since 1844, human beings have been living in the time of the investigative judgment mentioned in Revelation 14:7 (GC 425).

Ellen White outlined three distinct periods related to the end time: (1) the time of the investigative or pre-Advent judgment, which concludes with the close of probation; (2) the great time of trouble, which follows the close of probation and concludes with the Second Advent; and (3) the millennium, which follows the Second Advent and concludes with the resurrection of the wicked, their final destruction in the lake of fire, and the creation of a new earth.

Events during the investigative judgment

In her visions, Ellen White was shown that the following events will take place during the period prior to the close of probation: In heaven, the investigative judgment will deal with those whose names are found in the book of life. On earth, a short time prior to the close of probation, religious and political leaders will form an image to the beast, and they will issue a universal Sunday law that will culminate in a death decree for God's true followers and the reception of the mark of the beast by those who oppose Him. This period is designated the early time of trouble. During this time, God's church will give the loud cry and will experience the latter rain, the shaking, the sealing, and a revival and reformation within the church such as has not been seen since the time of the early church, the original Pentecost.

Many of these events may happen simultaneously. Ellen White didn't provide a chronological sequence for their occurrence. However, when the decree of Revelation 22:11 is issued, all these events will be finished and the great time of trouble will begin. While Mrs. White didn't specify what length of time these events will occupy, she did say that "the final movements will be rapid ones" (9T 11).

1. Revival and reformation in the church. Revival and reformation in the remnant church prepares it for the final events and the giving of the loud cry. There will be a revival of primitive godliness such "as has not been witnessed since apostolic times" (GC 464). Characteristics of this revival and reformation will include miracles of healing and genuine conversions (9T 126).

2. The sealing. In order to prepare His children for the time of trouble, God wants to seal them in their foreheads. This "is not any seal or mark that can be seen, but a settling into the truth, both intellectually and spiritually, so they cannot be moved" (4BC 1161) when the time of trouble comes.

3. The latter rain. The "latter rain" is promised in Joel 2:23, 28, 29. Just as the apostolic church received the early rain at Pentecost, so the remnant church will receive the latter rain, which will enable it to finish the work (see GC 611). This promise is not only for the future; it is for us today as well. However, we have to be ready to receive it. To be ready, we must put away all sin and seek the Lord in humility (see TM 507).

4. The loud cry. The message of the fall of Babylon (see Revelation 14:8) is repeated by the angel pictured in Revelation 18:1-4. This angel joins in the last great work of the third angel's message as it swells to a loud cry (see EW 277).

5. The shaking. This term refers to the shaking of God's people. It will be caused by the straight testimony of the True Witness to Laodicea (see EW 270) and by the introduction of false theories (see TM 112). Many Adventists will leave the church because they are not fully converted (see 4T 89).

6. The early time of trouble. The world and the church will experience a time of trouble before the close of probation. Political, financial, and social problems will increase (see Luke 21:25). Ellen White refers to this time in *Early Writings* (page 33). She says, "At the commencement of the time of trouble, we were filled with the Holy Ghost as we went forth and proclaimed the Sabbath more fully." Later on in the book she explains that the "commencement of the time of trouble" doesn't refer to the time when the plagues begin to be poured out but to a short period while Christ is still in the sanctuary just before the plagues begin. "At that time, while the work of salvation is closing, trouble will be coming on the earth, and the nations will be angry, yet held in check so as not to prevent the work of the third angel" (EW 85, 86).

7. The image of the beast. The image of the beast will be formed when the Protestant churches in America unite with the state to use its power to enforce their decrees and sustain the institutions of the church. "Then will Protestant America have formed an image to the Papacy [the beast], and there will be a national apostasy which will end only in national ruin" (ST, March 22, 1910).

8. Sunday laws. Revelation 13 predicts that in the future, there will be national and even international Sunday laws, and these laws will include religious observances. Revelation 13:3 also prophesies that "all the world . . . followed the beast." According to Ellen White, this means that "as America, the land of religious liberty, shall unite with the papacy in forcing the conscience and compelling men to honor the false sabbath, the people of *every country on the globe* will be led to follow her example" (6T 18, emphasis added).

9. Death decree. Seventh-day Adventist interpreters disagree regarding the timing of the death decree. Revelation 13:15 indicates that at some point during the final conflict a religious law will be passed that will carry the death penalty. Revelation 20:4 supports this by implication. It indicates that there will be martyrs in the final crisis who have not worshiped the beast or his image. "If there are to be martyrs over the mark of the beast issue obviously the enforcing of the mark of the beast must be done prior to these martyrdoms being carried out."[1] Since there will be no martyrs after the close of probation (see GC 634), the martyrs referred to in Revelation 20:4 must suffer their martyrdom before the close of probation. Consequently, we can conclude that the death decree must be issued before the close of probation.

A number of statements in Ellen G. White's writings support this interpretation: "When this time of trouble comes, every case is decided; there is no longer probation, no longer mercy for the impenitent. The seal of the living God is upon His people. This small remnant, unable to defend itself in the deadly conflict with the powers of earth that are marshaled by the dragon host, make God their defense. *The decree has been passed* by the highest earthly authority that they shall worship the beast and receive his mark under pain of persecution and death" (5T 213, emphasis added). This clearly indicates that when the time of trouble comes, probation is closed and the death decree "has been passed." In another place, Ellen White pictures Satan as saying, " 'When death shall be made the penalty of violating our sabbath, then many who are now ranked with commandment keepers will come over to our side' " (TM 473). Since there will be no changing of sides after the close of probation, the test involving a death threat must come before the close of probation.*

10. The mark of the beast. From the beginning, Seventh-day Adventists have connected Revelation's mark of the beast with state-enforced Sunday observance as a token of submission to Rome (see GC 449). However, "No one has yet received the mark of the beast. The testing time has not yet come" (Ev 234).

11. The close of probation. Human probation will close when Christ ends His ministry in heaven. The work of investigation and judgment will be finished, and the door of mercy will be shut (see GC 428). When Christ proclaims, "He that is unjust, let him be unjust still: . . . and he that is holy, let him be holy still" (Revelation 22:11, KJV), then "The seal of the living God is upon His people" (5T 212).

Events during the great time of trouble

Ellen White saw the great time of trouble, the outpouring of the seven last plagues, and the time of Jacob's trouble as following the close of probation. This great time of trouble climaxes in the battle of Armageddon during the sixth plague. Just prior to Christ's appearance in the clouds of heaven, a partial resurrection will occur (see Daniel 12:2). A short time later, at the second advent of Christ, the first resurrection and the translation of the righteous takes place.

* In *Early Writings,* 36, 37, Ellen White seems to place the death decree after the close of probation. However, this passage presents a condensed picture of final events that needs the elaboration and explanation provided by other passages and later statements. In *Early Writings,* she is viewing all the plagues before and after the close of probation as, in a sense, one. She condenses the picture in which the falling of such visitations stirs up the wicked. (Another possibility, which L. P. Tolhurst promotes, is that there will be two death decrees, one before and one after the close of probation [see L. P. Tolhurst, "The Death Decree in the Setting of the Final Crisis," unpublished MS, 10].)

The End-time Prophet and End-time Events

1. The time of Jacob's trouble. The time of Jacob's trouble, referred to in Jeremiah 30:7, begins with the death decree before the close of probation, but it occupies most of the great time of trouble. As Jacob wrestled with God even after he had confessed his sins (see Genesis 32), so God's people will experience a time of anguish and feel a deep sense of their unworthiness after the close of probation. However, "Their sins have gone beforehand to Judgment, and have been blotted out; and they cannot bring them to remembrance" (GC 620).

2. The great time of trouble (Daniel 12:1). The great time of trouble begins with the close of probation. During this time, the seven last plagues will fall on the earth. God's long-suffering has ended. The wicked have passed the boundary of their probation, and the Spirit of God has been at last withdrawn. "Satan will then plunge the inhabitants of the earth into one great, final trouble" (GC 614).

3. Armageddon (Revelation 16:12-16). The three unclean spirits (spirits of demons) come out of the mouth of the dragon (spiritualism), the beast (the papacy), and the false prophet (apostate Protestantism). They arm the powers of this world for a final battle against God and His people. Armageddon takes place wherever God's people are endangered by the enemy. At the time of their greatest danger, however, Jesus appears in the clouds of heaven to rescue them (see EW 284).

4. Special resurrection. Just before the appearance of Christ, there is a special resurrection (see Daniel 12:2; Revelation 1:7). All who participated in the crucifixion of Christ, the greatest enemies of the truth through the ages, and all those who died believing in the third angel's message will be resurrected to see Jesus come in the clouds of heaven (see GC 637).

5. The Second Coming. When Christ returns, the first general resurrection—the resurrection of the righteous dead—takes place (see Revelation 20:4, 5; GC 644), the living who have accepted Jesus as their Savior are translated (see 1 Thessalonians 4:17; GC 645), and the unbelievers are destroyed (see 2 Thessalonians 2:8; DA 107). At that time the millennium will commence.

Events related to the millennium

Ellen White describes the millennium as the period during which the wicked will be judged. During this time, Satan and his angels are bound here on earth, and the earth is devastated and in ruins. At the end of this period, the wicked are resurrected and Satan leads them in a final attempt to overthrow the rule of God in the Holy City, but he and his followers are destroyed by fire from heaven. These events are followed by the re-creation of the earth as the home of the redeemed.

1. Judgment of the wicked. During the millennium, between the first and the second resurrections, the judgment of the wicked takes place. It is at this time that "the saints shall judge the world" (1 Corinthians 6:2, 3, KJV). "In union with Christ they judge the wicked, comparing their acts with the statute book, the Bible, and deciding every case according to the deeds done in the body" (FLB 216).

2. The earth in ruins and Satan is bound. During the millennium, the earth is devastated and desolate. John calls it "the bottomless pit" (Revelation 20:3). Ellen White identifies this description with "the earth in a state of confusion and darkness" during the millennium (GC 658). This desolate planet is to be the home of Satan with his evil angels for a thousand years. Limited to the earth, he won't have access to other worlds to tempt their inhabitants. "It is in this sense that he is bound: there are none remaining, upon whom he can exercise his power. He is wholly cut off from the work of deception and ruin which for so many centuries has been his sole delight" (GC 659).

3. Resurrection of the wicked. At the end of the millennium, Jesus returns again to this earth. Ellen White describes His descent upon the Mount of Olives. "As his feet touch the mountain," she says, "it parts asunder, and becomes a very great plain, and is prepared for the reception of the holy city in which is the paradise of God, the garden of Eden, which was taken up after man's transgression" (3SG 84, 85). The City of God comes down and settles upon the plain prepared for it. Then Jesus leaves the city and calls forth the wicked dead. "All come up as they went down into their graves" (ibid.).

4. Satan's final battle against God. As the wicked come forth from their graves, Ellen White says, "they resume the current of their thoughts where it ceased in death. They possess the same desire to conquer which ruled when they fell" (EW 293). They "bear the traces of disease and death" (GC 662). Satan deceives them into attacking the Holy City, but fire rains upon them, and they are all consumed together.

5. The new earth. The fire that consumes the wicked will purify the earth. God will sweep away every trace of the curse and make the earth new (see

GC 674). The great controversy is ended. Sin and sinners are no more. The entire universe is clean. Then all things animate and inanimate will forever declare that God is love (see GC 678).

Ellen White's inspired teaching about end-time events must be seen from the perspective of the great controversy, in which salvation by faith in Christ is the central focus. The issue in the final confrontation between good and evil is not simply that of keeping God's law. The law reveals the justification of the saints; their obedience is the outward sign that Christ's righteousness has been imputed and imparted to them.

CHAPTER

Interpreting the Prophetic Writings

As Seventh-day Adventists, we believe that the Seventh-day Adventist Church is the remnant church of Revelation 12:17 and that God has graciously given this church a special gift, the gift of prophecy as manifested in the life and work of Ellen White. Since we don't believe in degrees of inspiration, we have to recognize that Mrs. White's inspiration is equal to that of the Old and New Testament prophets (though she didn't have equal authority). Therefore, when using and interpreting what she has written, we must apply the same principles of interpretation to her writings as we do to Scripture. Both are inspired literature; therefore, both must be interpreted by the same principles.

Biblical texts can be understood and used in different ways. People may want to know what the author intended to say when he or she wrote the text. Thus they will investigate the historical circumstances that led to the writing of the text, to whom it was addressed, and what the words in the original language really meant. This investigation is called exegesis.

Or a preacher may just want to use the language of a text in a worship setting, applying the text to a present-day problem or situation, even though when the text was written—in other words, in its historical context—it may have referred to a different situation and may have meant something quite different. This application is called the homiletical use of Scripture.

Here's an example of the homiletical use of Scripture: Mark 1:15 says that Jesus came to Galilee preaching the gospel, and saying, " 'The time is fulfilled, and the kingdom of God is at hand. Repent, and believe in the gospel.' " The kingdom that Jesus was proclaiming at that time was the kingdom of grace, which He established at His first advent.* However, we can also apply the text to our situation today. All the time prophecies have been fulfilled, the kingdom of God is at hand, and we need to repent and believe the gospel. The kingdom in this application, however, is the kingdom of glory that Christ will inaugurate at His second coming, not the kingdom of grace. The first interpretation of Mark 1:15 is called exegetical; the second, homiletical. Both uses are legitimate, but we must distinguish between them. And any teaching or doctrine of Scripture must be based on a careful exegesis of the text, not on a homiletical application of it.

Ellen White's use of Scripture

Ellen White frequently used Scripture homiletically.† She was steeped in the language of the Bible, and whenever she spoke or wrote on a topic, she would use biblical language and biblical texts to convey the message she had received. For example, in the book *The Great Controversy,* Ellen White wrote, "Those who accept the teachings of God's Word will not be wholly ignorant concerning the heavenly abode. And yet, 'eye hath not seen, nor ear heard, neither have entered into the heart of man, the things which God hath prepared for them that love him.' [1 COR. 2:9.] Human language is inadequate to describe the reward of the righteous. It will be known only to those who behold it. No finite mind can comprehend the glory of the Paradise of God" (GC 675).

In this passage Ellen White applied 1 Corinthians 2:9 to the new earth. When we study the verse in its context, however, we discover that Paul was not speaking about the new earth but about the Cross and salvation (see 1 Corinthians 2:1-8). Ellen White used the language of the verse and applied it to the new earth because what it says is true of the new earth as well—no eye has seen and no ear heard what God has prepared for His people.

---

* "The kingdom of grace was instituted immediately after the fall of man. . . . Yet it was not actually established until the death of Christ." Ellen G. White, *God's Amazing Grace* (Washington, D.C.: Review and Herald®, 1973), 19.

† This has been recognized for a long time. In 1981, Robert W. Olson, director of the Ellen G. White Estate, wrote, "Ellen White's writings are generally homiletical or evangelistic in nature and not strictly exegetical." Robert W. Olson, *One Hundred and One Questions on the Sanctuary and Ellen White* (Washington D.C.: Ellen G. White Estate, 1981), 41.

Reading through the books of Ellen White, we come across many other examples in which she used the language of a biblical verse or passage to express the message God gave her for the church. The fact that she used these texts doesn't mean that she was thereby interpreting them—she wasn't necessarily explaining what the biblical author meant to say. The meaning the original author intended the text to have may be quite different from the message Ellen White was conveying through her use of the text's language. Raoul Dederen aptly observed, "As interpreter of the Bible, Ellen White's most characteristic role was that of an evangelist—not an exegete, nor a theologian, as such, but a preacher and an evangelist. . . .

. . . The prophetic and hortatory mode was more characteristic of her than the exegetical. . . . The people to whom she was preaching—or writing—were more the object of her attention than the specific people to whom the individual Bible writers addressed themselves."[1]

Some people try to use Ellen White's writings as the last word on the meaning of a particular text. That's when understanding how she's using the text is particularly important.

Interpreting the Ellen G. White writings

We could avoid much controversy and misunderstanding if, in interpreting and applying the writings of Ellen G. White, besides paying attention to how she used Scripture, we always observe the following four basic guidelines.

1. Consider the historical context. In Ellen White's opening address at the 1901 General Conference in Battle Creek, she spoke of the need to reorganize the General Conference. "There are to be more than one or two or three men to consider the whole vast field," she said. "God has not put any kingly power in our ranks to control this or that branch of the work. The work has been greatly restricted by the efforts to control it in every line." She called for a complete "reorganization; a power and strength must be brought into the committees that are necessary" (LDE 53).

What had happened that occasioned these strong statements? When we look at the development of our church during the last few decades of the nineteenth century, we find that while the General Conference Executive Committee had thirteen members, six of the thirteen were spread out across North America and two resided overseas, so the full committee didn't often meet. Thus the five members of the committee who lived in Battle Creek, together with the secretary and the treasurer of the General Conference, who were not members of the committee, "carried the day-to-day responsibilities of the operation of the church."[2] Therefore, in her opening address at that General Conference session, Ellen White told the delegates, "That these men should stand in a sacred place, to be as the voice of God to the people, as we once believed the General Conference to be,—that is past. What we want now is a reorganization" (GCB, April 3, 1901 par. 25).

Ellen White's appeal didn't go unheeded. The delegates to that General Conference session effected a reorganization that largely corrected the "kingly power" problem. The General Conference Committee was enlarged to twenty-five members, the various independent organizations became departments of the General Conference, and the newly formed union conferences took over the day-to-day running of their fields. A few months

later, Ellen White wrote, "During the General Conference the Lord wrought mightily for His people. Every time I think of that meeting, a sweet solemnity comes over me, and sends a glow of gratitude to my soul" (RH, Nov. 26, 1901; LDE 54).

In that same year, her son Edson, who had run into difficulties with the Review and Herald publishing house prior to the 1888 Minneapolis General Conference, sought compensation from the church leadership. In presenting his case, he quoted from his mother's pre-1901 writings. When she heard what Edson had done, she wrote to him,

Edson J. White (1849–1928)

I am again much burdened as I see you selecting words from writings that I have sent you, and using them to force decisions that the brethren do not regard with clearness. I have received letters from Elder Daniells and Elder Kilgore asking me to send them instruction at once, if I have any light in reference to the points you have quoted from my letters.

Your course would have been the course to be pursued if no change had been made in the General Conference. But a change has been made, and many more changes will be made and great developments will be seen. No issues are to be forced (19MR 146).

The situation had changed, and she didn't want her pre-1901 statements applied to the new situation at the General Conference.

So, we need to look at the historical context—the time, place, and circumstances under which a particular statement was written. Unless there are valid reasons for doing so, we cannot make into a universal statement applicable at all times what Ellen White wrote addressing a particular situation in her time.

2. Study the immediate context. The immediate context is what comes immediately before and after a particular statement. What was Ellen White referring to in the paragraph or chapter from which a statement is taken?

In the book *Christ's Object Lessons,* Ellen White said, "Those who accept the Saviour, however sincere their conversion, should never be taught to say or to feel that they are saved" (COL 155). Many Christians then and now have believed in the erroneous doctrine of "once saved, always saved." Ellen White clearly opposed this teaching. In the immediate context, she said,

> There is nothing so offensive to God or so dangerous to the human soul as pride and self-sufficiency. Of all sins it is the most hopeless, the most incurable.
>
> Peter's fall was not instantaneous, but gradual. Self-confidence led him to the belief that he was saved, and step after step was taken in the downward path, until he could deny his Master. Never can we safely put confidence in self or feel, this side of heaven, that we are secure against temptation. Those who accept the Saviour, however sincere their conversion, should never be taught to say or to feel that they are saved. This is misleading. Every one should be taught to cherish hope and faith; but even when we give ourselves to Christ and know that He accepts us, we are not beyond the reach of temptation (ibid., 154, 155).

The context makes it clear that she is addressing the issue of self-confidence and temptations after conversion. We are never secure against temptations; we can never say that we cannot fall—that we are saved and therefore secure from temptation. But this doesn't mean that day by day we cannot have the assurance of salvation (see 1 John 5:12, 13). As Ellen White herself noted in the above statement, we may "give ourselves to Christ and know that He accepts us."

3. Study the larger context. The "larger context" refers to other statements Ellen White has written on a particular topic. To illustrate this principle, we will look at one aspect of the Adventist health message: meat eating. On this issue, Mrs. White made some very absolute-sounding statements. But she also made many modifying statements that we need to consider before we draw any conclusions regarding this topic.

In 1903, Ellen White made what seems to be quite an absolute statement. She wrote, "Vegetables, fruits, and grains should compose our diet. Not an ounce of flesh meat should enter our stomachs. The eating of flesh is unnatural. We are to return to God's original purpose in the creation of man" (CD 380). Anyone reading this statement by itself would have to conclude that under no circumstances are we to eat meat.

However, just a few pages further on in the book, we find a modifying statement from the year 1890 on the same topic.

Where plenty of good milk and fruit can be obtained there is rarely any excuse for eating animal food; it is not necessary to take the life of any of God's creatures to supply our ordinary needs. In certain cases of illness or exhaustion it may be thought best to use some meat, but great care should be taken to secure the flesh of healthy animals. It has come to be a very serious question whether it is safe to use flesh food at all in this age of the world. It would be better never to eat meat than to use the flesh of animals that are not healthy. When I could not obtain the food I needed, I have sometimes eaten a little meat; but I am becoming more and more afraid of it (ibid., 394).

The modifying circumstances she referred to are cases of illness or when other food is not readily available. She admitted that she herself ate meat from time to time. Therefore, in a very balanced statement made before the delegates at the General Conference in 1909, she said, "We do not mark out any precise line to be followed in diet; but we do say that in countries where there are fruits, grains, and nuts in abundance, flesh food is not the right food for God's people. . . . If meat eating was ever healthful, it is not safe now. Cancers, tumors, and pulmonary diseases are largely caused by meat eating.

"We are not to make the use of flesh food a test of fellowship, but we should consider the influence that professed believers who use flesh foods have over others" (9T 159).

We should certainly aim for a vegetarian diet, but we should never make it a test of fellowship. In some circumstances, a diet that includes some meat may even be the best, but this should never serve as an excuse to continue eating meat when there is no real necessity. "A meat diet is not the most wholesome of diets, and yet I would not take the position that meat should be discarded by every one. Those who have feeble digestive organs can often use meat, when they cannot eat vegetables, fruit, or porridge" (CD 394, 395).

When we look at the total body of what Ellen White has written on a given topic, a balanced picture emerges that is invaluable for all Christians who take their religion seriously, and particularly for Seventh-day Adventists, whom God has called to be His witnesses in these last days.

4. Look for principles. Prophets convey God's truth as principles or policies. Principles are universal and apply to all people, in all places, and at all times. Policies are the applications of principles to particular situations. Policies may change as circumstances change; they may look different in different cultures and places. "That which can be said of men under certain circumstances cannot be said of them under other circumstances" (3T 470). Two examples from the writings of Ellen White come readily to mind.

First, in 1903, at a time when cars were not yet generally available, Ellen White wrote, "If girls, . . . could learn to harness and drive a horse, and to use the saw and the hammer, as well as the rake and the hoe, they would be better fitted to meet the emergencies of life" (Ed 216). The principle in this statement is that girls should be "fitted to meet the emergencies of life." Applied to our time, it could mean that girls should learn how to drive and look after a car.

And second, in 1895, while Ellen White was in Australia, she was given a view of happenings in Battle Creek. Among the scenes shown to her was one involving bicycles used for racing. At the end of the nineteenth century, the bicycle was not an economical means of transportation. Rather, it was a rich man's toy. The best early bicycles cost $150, an amount comparable to the cost of an expensive car today. People were mortgaging their income for months in advance to buy what was then an expensive luxury item.

On February 6, 1896, Ellen White wrote a letter to the church members in Battle Creek in which, among many other things, she said, "The money expended in bicycles and dress and other needless things must be accounted for. . . . As God's people you should represent Jesus; but Christ is ashamed of the self-indulgent ones. My heart is pained, I can scarcely restrain my feelings, when I think how easily our people are led away from practical Christian principles to self-pleasing" (TM 398).

Within a few years' time, the bicycle became a useful and inexpensive means of transportation, and Ellen White never commented on it again. Her policy on bicycles was based on the biblical principle of good stewardship. If she were alive today, doubtless she would apply this principle to the way people spend money on cars, boats, electronic gadgets, etc.

In summary, context is all important. In our interpretation of the writings of Ellen White, the historical and literary context will help us to navigate safely between the Scylla and Charybdis of too literal an interpretation on one hand and, on the other, an interpretation that is so far removed from the intent of the author that it is useless.

Ellen G. White's growth

In addition to the principles of interpretation listed above, we need to remember that prophets don't necessarily receive all the light at once. They experience growth in their understanding of heavenly things. In Daniel 8:27, the prophet says, "I was appalled by the vision and did not understand it" (RSV). About ten years later, the angel Gabriel came and explained to Daniel the full import of the vision.

Similarly, Ellen White experienced growth in her understanding of what God revealed to her. In 1904 she wrote, "Often representations are given me which at first I do not understand, but after a time they are made plain by a repeated presentation of those things that I did not at first comprehend, and in ways that make their meaning clear and unmistakable" (3SM 56).

When we compare earlier writings of Ellen White with her later works, we find that she at times modified, expanded, or shortened her earlier writings, reflecting a deeper insight into God's messages. This can best be illustrated by her treatment of the great controversy theme in the course of her ministry.

Ellen White's two-hour vision at Lovett's Grove, Ohio, in 1858 became known as the "Great Controversy vision." The first account of what she saw in this vision appeared in 1858 in 219 pages in *Spiritual Gifts,* volume 1. The 460 pages of *Spiritual Gifts,* volumes 3 and 4, published in 1864 enlarged on the great controversy theme in the Old Testament. This was followed by the four-volume *Spirit of Prophecy* series, published between 1870 and 1884, that presented a much more detailed account of the great controversy story in a total of 1,696 pages of text. In time, the four *Spirit of Prophecy* volumes were replaced by the five volumes of the Conflict of the Ages series, which, in 3,507 pages, recounts in even greater detail the great controversy story. As Mrs. White developed this important theme over the course of her lifetime, she modified and expanded it under the guidance of the Holy Spirit. Her understanding of this issue came to permeate almost all her books, even those that on the surface deal with other matters, such as the books *Education* and *The Ministry of Healing.*

Ellen G. White as a historian

Prophets are God's mouthpieces—they aren't scientists or historians. Thus it happened that in using history books Ellen White inadvertently incorporated some of the historical errors contained in those books into her own writings, and God didn't see fit to give her a vision to correct those errors. This, however, doesn't detract from her inspiration or her authority, just as historical errors in Scripture don't detract from its inspiration or authority.

For example, in Acts 7:16, Stephen says that Abraham bought the cave of Machpelah from Hamor, the father of Shechem. When we read the account of this purchase in Genesis 23:7-17, however, we discover that Abraham bought the cave not from Hamor but from Ephron the Hittite.[*] Yet God didn't see fit to correct Luke. Nor did He correct Matthew when that disciple wrote that the words " 'And they took the thirty pieces of silver' " are from Jeremiah, though they're really from Zechariah (see Matthew 27:9; Zechariah 11:12, 13). God obviously didn't consider these historical details sufficiently important to give a vision to correct them.

In 1912, W. C. White wrote a letter to S. N. Haskell in which he stated that Ellen White had

---

[*] Furthermore, from Genesis 33:18, 19, we learn that Jacob bought his plot of land from the children of Hamor, the father of Shechem.

never wished our brethren to treat them [her writings] as authority on history. When "Great Controversy" was first written, she often times gave a partial description of some scene presented to her, and when Sister Davis made inquiry regarding time and place, Mother referred her to what was already written in the book of Elder Smith and in secular histories. When "Controversy" was written, Mother never thought that the readers would take it as an authority on historical dates and use it to settle controversies, and she does not now feel that it ought to be used in that way.[3]

At the end of this letter, Ellen White wrote, "I approve of the remarks made in this letter" and signed her name.[4]

In view of Mrs. White's own understanding of this matter, we should be careful about trying to use the historical narratives in her books to settle details of history.* This, of course, doesn't mean that we can push Creation back tens of thousands or millions of years, or that the prophetic dates like 1798 or 1844 can be changed. In regard to the age of the earth, she wrote, "Infidel geologists claim that the world is very much older than the Bible record makes it. They reject the Bible record, because of those things which are to them evidences from the earth itself, that the world has existed tens of thousands of years" (3SG 91). She herself always referred to the age of the earth in terms of about six thousand years (see PP 51; DA 413; etc.).

So, by applying a few simple principles of interpretation, we can gain a clearer, more accurate view of God's will for us.

---

* At issue here are details—not milestones—of history. When *The Great Controversy* was revised in 1911, a number of historical details were stated more precisely. For example, regarding the persecution of the Waldenses by the Roman Catholic Church, the 1888 edition had the sentence, "Everything heretical, whether persons or writings, was destroyed," giving the impression that all the Waldenses were destroyed. The 1911 edition reads, "Everything heretical, whether persons or writings, she [the church] sought to destroy" (GC 62).

CHAPTER

The Blessings of the Prophetic Gift

In the winter of 1849–1850, James and Ellen White were laboring for souls in Oswego, New York.[1] While they were there, a revival was started in one of the Protestant churches by a layman who was the county treasurer. This man seemed to have a great burden for the unconverted.

A young man, Hiram Patch, and his fiancée were wondering whether they should cast their lot with the revival or join with the Sabbath keeping Adventists. In vision Ellen White was shown the true character of the man conducting the revival, and she told Hiram Patch that she had been instructed to say to him, "Wait a month, and you will know for yourself the character of the persons who are engaged in this revival, and who profess to have such a great burden for sinners. He has no real burden for sinners." At this Mr. Patch replied, "I will wait."

Two weeks later, a blood vessel burst in the stomach of the treasurer-revivalist, and he was confined to his bed. When others took over his work at the county office, they discovered that the county funds were a thousand dollars short. An inquiry made by the sheriff brought only solemn denials from the treasurer of any knowledge about the missing money—until another officer observed the treasurer's wife hastily hiding something in a snowbank and found it to be a bag containing the money. Needless to say, the revival collapsed, and Hiram Patch and his fiancée, with the words of the prediction still fresh in their ears, became fruitful members of the remnant church. This experience of a prediction fulfilled within two weeks after the words were spoken inspired confidence in the hearts of the onlookers.

Not only was Ellen White's counsel helpful to many individuals with whom she came in contact, but her many contributions to the Seventh-day Adventist Church have been invaluable. She helped the church grow in recognition of its God-given mission; in the educational, health, and publishing branches of its work; and in meeting theological challenges.

Mission

In the early decades of our history, most Adventists believed that the church was fulfilling God's command to teach all nations by preaching to the many immigrants in North America. In response to a reader's letter, Uriah Smith wrote in 1859, "We have no information that the Third [Angel's] Message is at present being proclaimed in any country besides our own. . . . Our own land is composed of people from almost every nation."[2]

Five years later, M. B. Czechowski volunteered to go as a missionary to Europe, but the church turned down his request for their support. Czechowski then asked the support of the first-day Adventists, and they sent him to Europe, where he preached the three angels' messages and established Seventh-day Adventist companies. In the meantime, Ellen White educated the church about its worldwide responsibility. In 1871, she wrote, "Much can be done through the medium of the press, but still more can be accomplished if the influence of the labors of the living preachers goes with our publications. . . .

"When the churches see young men possessing zeal to qualify themselves to extend their labors to cities, villages, and towns that have never been aroused to the truth, and missionaries volunteering to go to other nations to carry the truth to them, the churches will be encouraged and strengthened" (LS 205).

In 1874, she had an impressive dream about giving the third angel's message to the world. In the dream she was told, " 'You are entertaining too limited ideas of the work for this time. You are trying to plan the work so that you can embrace it in your arms. You must take broader views. Your light must not be put under a bushel or under a bed, but on a candlestick, that it may give light to all that are in the house. Your house is the world. . . .

. . . " 'The message will go in power to all parts of the world, to Oregon, to Europe, to Australia, to the islands of the sea, to all nations, tongues, and peoples' " (ibid., 208, 209).

That same year, J. N. Andrews became the first official Seventh-day Adventist missionary. He and his children went to Switzerland, and three years later, the John G. Matteson family was sent to Scandinavia. By 1890, there were Adventist missionaries in eighteen countries. And today, Seventh-day Adventists have an established work in 204 of the 229 countries of the world recognized by the United Nations.

Education

In 1872, Ellen White received a vision on proper principles of education. A short time later, she wrote thirty pages recording what she had been told. Among other things, she wrote, "We need a school where those who

John N. Andrews (1829–1883)

are just entering the ministry may be taught at least the common branches of education and where they may also learn more perfectly the truths of God's word for this time" (3T 160).

Battle Creek College was officially opened two years later, and soon it offered bachelor degrees in arts and science. At first, the curriculum mirrored the classical education pattern that the state colleges followed at that time. This meant that Bachelor of Arts students studied three years each of classical Latin and Greek, and science students took four years of Latin and two years of Greek. The students had to read Virgil, Ovid, Cicero, Seneca, Xenophon, Demosthenes, Homer, and other pagan authors.[3] Furthermore, except for the mission course, the majors offered didn't require any Bible classes. Thus in 1877–1878, for instance, the college had an enrollment of 413 students but only 75 took a Bible class.[4]

For years Ellen White urged that the Bible and not infidel authors should be the center of our educational program. In 1896, she wrote, "The greatest wisdom, and most essential, is the knowledge of God. Self sinks into insignificance as it contemplates God and Jesus Christ whom He hath sent. The

Bible must be made the foundation for all study" (FE 451). A year later, E. A. Sutherland became president of the college, and the classical curriculum was abolished. From 1898 on, only New Testament Greek, New Testament Latin, and medical Latin were taught.

Today, Seventh-day Adventists have 5,500 schools and about 100 colleges and universities around the globe. We have the largest Protestant school system in the world. Why? Because our pioneers took seriously what God told them through the gift of prophecy.

Health and medical work

Joseph Bates had become committed to living healthfully prior to 1843, but during the first twenty years of our history, the rest of our pioneers were anything but health reformers. At the 1848 Sabbath conferences we have to imagine our pioneers chewing tobacco while they studied the Bible and eating pork chops for lunch. Health reform was not on their agenda.

In the autumn of 1848, Ellen White was shown that tobacco, tea, and coffee are harmful, but no special effort was made "to induce Sabbathkeeping Adventists to discontinue the use of tobacco until the latter part of 1853."[5] Two years later, it was decided to disfellowship people who refused to give up tobacco.[6]

On June 6, 1863, Ellen White received a forty-five-minute vision in Otsego, Michigan, in which she was shown the need for health reform. "I saw that it was a sacred duty to attend to our health, and arouse others to their duty, . . . we have a duty to speak, to come out against intemperance of every kind,—intemperance in working, in eating, in drinking and in drugging— and then point them to God's great medicine, water, pure soft water, for diseases, for health, for cleanliness, and for a luxury. . . .

"I saw that we should not be silent upon the subject of health but should wake up minds to the subject" (3SM 280).

Two years later, on December 25, 1865, Mrs. White had a vision in Rochester, New York, in which she was shown that Adventists "should provide a home for the afflicted and those who wish to learn how to take care of their bodies that they may prevent sickness. . . .

"Our people should have an institution of their own, under their own control, for the benefit of the diseased and suffering among us who wish to have health and strength that they may glorify God in their bodies and spirits, which are His" (1T 489–492). Nine months later, in September

1866, the Western Health Reform Institute, our first health institution, was opened in Battle Creek, Michigan. Today, Seventh-day Adventists operate more than seven hundred hospitals, clinics, and dispensaries around the world.

Many of the principles of healthful living found in the writings of Ellen White were already being taught in a limited way by other health reformers of her day. But in their teaching we find many errors and extremes—which Ellen White was able to avoid because of the instructions she received from God. For example, Sylvester Graham and James Jackson, two prominent nineteenth-century health reformers, both taught that people shouldn't eat salt. Mrs. White, however, wrote, "I use some salt, and always have, because salt, instead of being deleterious, is actually essential for the blood" (9T 162). And Ellen White avoided other erroneous beliefs of the nineteenth-century health reformers, such as that people shouldn't cut their hair, that they shouldn't drink water but get the liquid they need only from fruit, that the fat in meat offers the best nutrition, that people shouldn't use soap, and that overweight people are healthy people.[7]

As Ellen White introduced the subject of health to church members, some said to her, " 'You speak very nearly the opinions taught in the *Laws of Life,* and other publications, by Drs. Trall, Jackson, and others. Have you read that paper and those works?' " She replied that she had not read them, "neither should I read them till I had fully written out my views, lest it should be said that I have received my light upon the subject of health from physicians, and not from the Lord" (3SM 277).

Drs. Leonard Brand and Don S. McMahon note, "During the first half of the twentieth century, up to the late 1950s, medical and nutritional knowledge made Adventist health principles seem like an unfortunate mistake. For example, nutritionists considered a vegetarian diet very inadequate for maintaining good health. Since that time, research in medical and nutritional science has increased greatly, and it has reversed this opinion. Medical authorities now regard the Adventist lifestyle as the epitome of desirable lifestyles."[8]

While for the most part, current medical authorities commend the health practices Ellen White recommended to the church, some of the reasons she gave for the various health principles seem somewhat strange today. Dr. McMahon made a comparative study of the writings of Ellen White and those of other health reformers of her time. His study led him to the conclusion that she received the health principles she promoted (the "whats") through inspiration, as evidenced by the fact that without any medical education she was able to recognize valid concepts and reject faulty ones. But he came to believe that she often borrowed from her contemporaries the explanations or reasons (the "whys") for the principles that she taught. The reason for this, says McMahon, was that God "could not have explained some of the 'whys' correctly at that time without inventing medical vocabulary and revealing physiological concepts that were not known until decades after Ellen White wrote."[9]

Publishing

In November 1848, Ellen White had a vision in the home of Otis Nichol in Dorchester, Massachusetts. When she came out of the vision she said to her husband James, " 'I have a message for you. You must begin to print a little paper and send it out to the people. Let it be small at first; but as the people read, they will send you means with which to print, and it will be a success from the first. From this small beginning it was shown to me to be like streams of light that went clear round the world' " (LS 125).

"Streams of light . . . clear around the world"! How could that be? Jesus was coming soon. There were few Sabbath keeping Adventists, and none of them were great scholars or wealthy persons. Furthermore, the world was unbelieving. Yet this young woman predicted that a work of publishing to be started by her penniless husband would grow until it encompassed the globe.

More than half a year went by before James White could make even the smallest beginning. In the summer of 1849, he arranged for the printing, on credit, of a thousand copies of an eight-page paper called *Present Truth.* As Ellen White had been shown, enough funds did come in to defray the cost, and James White continued to publish the little paper, which in 1850 he renamed *The Second Advent Review and Sabbath Herald.* Today, Seventh-day Adventists publish literature in more than 270 languages in 57 publishing houses around the world.

Theology

More than once, Ellen White's counsel prevented the church from making serious theological errors.

Fanaticism. In the 1840s and 1850s, Mrs. White had to combat fanaticism of various kinds. Some people claimed to be perfect, others that no one should work anymore, and still others kept setting times for Christ's return.

There were some who professed great humility, and advocated creeping on the floor like children, as an evidence of their humility. They claimed that the words of Christ in Matthew 18:1-6 must have a literal fulfillment at this period, when they were looking for their Saviour to return. They would creep around their houses, on the street, over bridges, and in the church itself.

I told them plainly that this was not required; that the humility which God looked for in His people was to be shown by a Christlike life, not by creeping on the floor. All spiritual things are to be treated with sacred dignity. Humility and meekness are in accordance with the life of Christ, but they are to be shown in a dignified way (LS 85, 86).

Righteousness by faith. The 1888 General Conference in Minneapolis was marked by theological controversy. Until that meeting, most Seventh-day Adventists believed that by obeying the commandments with the help of the Holy Spirit, they could achieve righteousness acceptable to God. E. J. Waggoner and A. T. Jones, however, taught that even with the help of the Holy Spirit, humanity's obedience can never satisfy God's law; that Christ's imputed righteousness alone is the basis of our acceptance by God; and that we continually need the covering of Christ's righteousness, it is not just for our sins of the past.

John H. Kellogg (1852–1943)

Many people in leadership positions, including G. I. Butler, the General Conference president, and Uriah Smith, the editor of the *Review and Herald,* opposed this teaching. They feared it would undermine the law and the Sabbath. Ellen White's strong support for Waggoner and Jones at Minneapolis, however, saved the church from legalism.

Pantheism. At the 1903 Autumn Council, the General Conference Committee wrestled with the issue of pantheism in Dr. Kellogg's book *The Living Temple*. Pantheism teaches that God is not a personal being but the life force in all living things. After spending a whole day discussing the matter, Elder Daniells, the president of the General Conference, considered it to be time to adjourn the meeting, but he dared not call for a vote. People were too confused and uncertain, and he didn't wish to take a step that would solidify any conclusions. So he closed the session, and everyone went to their lodgings.

When Daniells arrived at his house, a group of people was waiting for

him. They appeared to be very happy, and one of them said, " 'Deliverance has come! Here are two messages from Mrs. White.' "

"No one can imagine," said Elder Daniells later, "the eagerness with which I read the documents that had come in the mail while we were in the midst of our discussions. There was a most positive testimony regarding the dangerous errors that were taught in 'The Living Temple.' "[10]

In the first letter, Ellen White had written, " 'I have some things to say to our teachers in reference to the new book *The Living Temple*. Be careful how you sustain

Arthur G. Daniells (1858–1935)

the sentiments of this book regarding the personality of God. As the Lord presents matters to me, these sentiments do not bear the endorsement of God. They are a snare that the enemy has prepared for these last days.' "[11]

In the second letter, she told Daniells, " 'After taking your position firmly, wisely, cautiously, make not one concession on any point concerning which God has plainly spoken. Be as calm as a summer evening, but as fixed as the everlasting hills.' "[12]

The next morning the delegates met again. After prayer, Brother Daniells rose and told the brethren that he had received two very important messages from Sister White. Everyone was curious to hear the letters, and they sat in thoughtful silence while he read them. As statement after statement setting forth the false teaching in the book *The Living Temple* was read, many loud "Amens" could be heard, and tears flowed freely.

With this, the matter was settled as far as the delegates were concerned. Even Dr. Kellogg promised to withdraw the book and to correct those parts that had raised objections; however, he never carried out this promise.

Why did this message come at exactly the right time? When Sister White received a letter of appreciation from Brother Daniells, she replied to him,

"Shortly before I sent the testimonies that you said arrived just in time, I had read an incident about a ship in a fog meeting an iceberg. For several nights I slept but little. I seemed to be bowed down as a cart beneath sheaves. One night a scene was clearly presented before me. A vessel was upon the waters, in a heavy fog. Suddenly the lookout cried, 'Iceberg just ahead!' There, towering high above the ship, was a gigantic iceberg. An authoritative voice cried out, 'Meet it!' There was not a moment's hesitation. It was a time for instant action. The engineer put on full steam, and the man at the wheel steered the ship straight into the iceberg. With a crash she struck the ice. There was a fearful shock, and the iceberg broke into many pieces, falling with a noise like thunder upon the deck. The passengers were violently shaken by the force of the collision, but no lives were lost. The vessel was injured, but not beyond repair. She rebounded from the contact, trembling from stem to stern, like a living creature. Then she moved forward on her way.

"Well I knew the meaning of this representation. I had my orders. I had heard the words, like a living voice from our Captain, 'Meet it!' I knew what my duty was, and that there was not a moment to lose. The time for decided action had come. I must without delay obey the command, 'Meet it!'

"This is why you received the testimonies when you did. That night I was up at one o'clock, writing as fast as my hand could pass over the paper."[13]

The guidance God has given the Seventh-day Adventist Church through the writings and counsel of Ellen G. White have blessed not only numerous individual members through the years but also the church and its institutions. This in itself comprises strong evidence that God worked through her in a special way.

Confidence in the Prophetic Gift

At the beginning of the twentieth century, Ellen White urged church leaders to establish sanitariums in several places in Southern California because thousands of tourists visited this region. In a vision in 1901, she had been shown a sanitarium outside of Los Angeles. In 1904, the church purchased facilities for Paradise Valley Sanitarium and Glendale Sanitarium, but neither of them fully matched the one she had seen in vision. So, Mrs. White encouraged the church leaders to keep looking.

In 1905, a health resort named Loma Linda was put on the market for $110,000. John Burden, manager of the Glendale Sanitarium, reported to Mrs. White that the seventy-six-acre property seemed to match her description but the price was too high. Sometime later, the price was reduced to $85,000, and Ellen White wrote to the church members in Southern California, "Arouse and avail yourselves of the opportunity open to you."

Soon afterward the price dropped further, to $45,000. Burden talked to the owners. They said if the church purchased the property within the next few days, they could have it for $40,000. Burden cabled Mrs. White asking for advice. Based on a vision she had received the night before, she asked her son Willie White to telegram him, telling him to secure the option to purchase the Loma Linda property. However, the members of the local conference committee were in Washington attending the General Conference session. They cabled John Burden to delay action until their return. What was he to do?

Convicted that it was the Lord's will that the property be secured, Ellen

Loma Linda

White urged Burden to go ahead and put down the deposit, which he did. But when the second installment of $5,000 was due and there was no money with which to make the payment, some felt that a mistake had been made. Then, a few hours before the deadline, a letter containing a bank draft for $5,000 arrived from a woman in Atlantic City. "I don't know just what your immediate need is, but if this will help, use it," the woman had written. Once again, God's guidance through Mrs. White was confirmed.[1]

Messenger to the remnant

William Foy (1818–1893), a black Freewill Baptist preacher, received at least three—possibly four—visions during the years 1842–1844. His first vision dealt with the reward of the righteous and the punishment of sinners, and the second with the coming judgment. At first he wasn't willing to relate to others what had been shown to him, but eventually he delivered the messages over several months in various churches. Young Ellen Harmon heard him speak once, at Beethoven Hall in Portland, Maine.

In Foy's third vision, given sometime during the summer of 1844, he saw a sequence of three platforms on which multitudes of people were gathered. The third platform extended to the gates of the Holy City. In his vision, he saw some people fall through the first and second platforms and disappear. These people, he was told, had apostatized. Foy stopped telling what he had been shown in this third vision—perhaps because he didn't understand what it meant.*

Just before the time of the Great Disappointment in 1844, God selected

---

* In 1858, Ellen White had a vision in which she was shown three steps, "the first, second, and third angels' messages" (EW 258)—possibly what Foy's third vision was about. In 1845, his first two visions were printed. (See William Foy, *The Christian Experience of William E. Foy Together With the Two Visions He Received in the Months of Jan. and Feb. 1842* [Portland, Maine: The Pearson Brothers, 1845].) According to Delbert W. Baker, although Foy didn't receive further visions, he lived until 1893 and "continued to pastor, preach, and hold revivals up to the time of his death." (Delbert W. Baker, *The Unknown Prophet* [Washington, D.C.: Review and Herald®, 1987], 130.)

another man as His spokesperson—a young Advent believer by the name of Hazen Foss, whose older brother had married Ellen Harmon's older sister Mary. Foss was shown the experience of the Advent people and their ultimate triumph, a vision similar to Ellen White's first one. After the Disappointment, he was bidden to relate to others what he had seen; but because of his discouragement that Christ hadn't returned as expected, he refused to accept the commission. Then he was told the burden would "be given to one of the weakest of the Lord's children, one who would faithfully relate what God would reveal."[2] When he changed his mind and wanted to relate what he had been shown, he could no longer remember the vision's content. A few weeks after the Great Disappointment, in December of 1844, Ellen Harmon received her first vision; and for the next seventy years she related to the members of the fledgling Seventh-day Adventist Church what God showed her in about two thousand dreams and visions.

Believe His prophet

Toward the end of the reign of King Jehoshaphat, the kings of Moab and Ammon united their armies to fight against Judah. Jehoshaphat proclaimed a fast throughout Judah and turned to the Lord in prayer. As the king and his people were humbling themselves before the Lord, through the gift of prophecy, Jehoshaphat received the assurance that the Lord would fight for the Judeans (see 2 Chronicles 20:1-18). Early the next morning, the king said to his people, " 'Hear me, O Judah and you inhabitants of Jerusalem: Believe in the LORD your God, and you shall be established; believe His prophets, and you shall prosper' " (verse 20). Then Jehoshaphat did something unusual; he told the temple singers to march ahead of the soldiers into battle. What a sight that must have been—the singers marching at the head of the army, lifting their voices in praise to God for the promised victory! And the Lord honored their faith. "When Judah came to a place overlooking the wilderness, they looked toward the multitude; and there were their dead bodies, fallen on the earth. No one had escaped" (verse 24).

"Believe in the LORD your God, and you shall be established; believe His prophets, and you shall prosper." The truth of this promise was brought home in a singular way to Australian Adventists in the 1890s. Soon after her arrival in Australia in 1891, Ellen White told the conference committee that the Lord had instructed her to tell them that they should establish a school. In response they pointed out that there were only about one thousand Adventists in all of Australia, few of whom owned their own homes. How could they purchase land, erect the necessary buildings, and establish, equip, and operate a school? While acknowledging the difficulties, Ellen White consistently reminded them of the school the Lord had shown her in vision.

Avondale

In 1894, the conference officials found in Cooranbong a block of fifteen hundred acres available for about three dollars an acre. The price seemed alluring, but the land itself was disappointing. Ellen White went with the committee to examine the property. Before starting out on the morning of the second day, they had a season of prayer. In the group that morning was an Elder McCullagh, who, afflicted with diseased lungs and throat, was losing ground physically. While they were all bowed in prayer, the Lord impressed Ellen White to pray for the healing of Brother McCullagh, which she did. Speaking of it later, he said that, as she prayed, it seemed as though a shock of electricity went through his body. His coughing ceased, he soon regained his strength, and he lived for many more years. The committee took this as a sign from God that they should move forward in faith and purchase the land. The experts they consulted, however, told them that the soil was poor and that they would be wasting their money purchasing the place. In a dream, Ellen White received another sign that she believed confirmed that in spite of what the land experts said, the Lord wanted them to purchase that property. Here is the remarkable story in her own words:

> Before I visited Cooranbong, the Lord gave me a dream. In my dream I was taken to the land that was for sale in Cooranbong. Several of our brethren had been solicited to visit the land, and I dreamed that as I was walking upon the ground I came to a neat cut furrow that had been ploughed one quarter of a yard deep, and two yards in length. Two of the brethren who had been acquainted with the rich soil of Iowa were standing before this furrow and saying, "This is not

good land; the soil is not favorable." But One who has often spoken in counsel was present also, and He said, "False witness has been borne of this land." Then He described the properties of the different layers of earth. He explained the science of the soil, and said that this land was adapted to the growth of fruit and vegetables, and that, if well worked, would produce its treasures for the benefit of man. This dream I related to Brother and Sister Starr and my family.

The next day we were on the cars, on our way to meet others who were investigating the land, and as I was afterward walking on the ground where the trees had been removed, lo, there was a furrow just as I had described it, and the men also who had criticized the appearance of the land. The words were spoken just as I had dreamed (8MR 259).

When Mrs. White told the members of her party what the angel had said in her dream, they were deeply impressed. They recognized that the Lord had indeed led them to this place, and they voted to purchase the property.

Time has vindicated the counsel Ellen White gave. The school prospered, becoming a model for Adventist schools around the globe, and it is still training young people for the Lord's work. It was this writer's privilege to spend three years at Avondale College in the 1960s and to witness firsthand how the Lord had blessed this school.

Opposition to Ellen White's ministry

As predicted in Scripture, the remnant church has been granted a manifestation of the prophetic gift in the life and work of Ellen G. White. Unfortunately, some people feel that although her messages were necessary to founding the church in the nineteenth century, they aren't relevant today. Others simply ignore her, reject her, or openly oppose her. She predicted all this. "The very last deception of Satan will be to make of none effect the testimony of the Spirit of God. . . . Satan will work ingeniously, in different ways and through different agencies, to unsettle the confidence of God's remnant people in the true testimony" (1SM 48).

Opposition or indifference to the writings of Ellen White usually is the result of one or more of the following:

• A failure to read enough of her writings to recognize and understand her overall, well-balanced instructions

- A failure to understand the proper relationship of her writings to Scripture
- A failure to recognize the true nature of divine inspiration
- A failure to recognize the principle of time and place in connection with the counsel she has given
- A failure to acknowledge that her counsels are still relevant today
- A failure to recognize that while sufficient evidence is given to convince the honest in heart, the Lord doesn't remove opportunities for doubt
- An unwillingness to sacrifice some cherished habit, practice, or belief that seems out of harmony with the counsels Ellen White has given

Most opposition to Ellen White's ministry would disappear

- if we would stop using some pet sentence or paragraph as a club with which to hit someone else.
- if we would apply the counsels to ourselves instead of trying to apply them to someone else.
- if we wouldn't "quote" her when we don't know where the quote is found. (There are many apocryphal sayings.)
- if we wouldn't discuss something she wrote without having studied everything she wrote on that particular topic. (Partial knowledge can be more dangerous than no knowledge at all.)
- if we would recognize that people's failure to live up to or carry out Ellen White's counsels has nothing whatsoever to do with the inspiration and reliability of those counsels.[3]

In 1870, J. N. Andrews wrote,

> The object of spiritual gifts is to maintain the living work of God in the church. They enable the Spirit of God to speak in the correction of wrongs, and in the exposure of iniquity. They are the means whereby God teaches his people when they are in danger of taking wrong steps. They are the means by which the Spirit of God sheds light upon church difficulties, when otherwise their adjustment would be impossible. . . . In short, their work is to unite the people of God in the same mind and in the same judgment upon the meaning of the Scriptures.[4]

A personal testimony

Although my mother was a firm believer in the Spirit of Prophecy, I had only a nodding acquaintance with Ellen White's books in my youth. At Newbold College in England I became better acquainted with her writings. But even there, like many other Europeans in those days, I had no particular interest in them. It wasn't until my wife and I emigrated with our firstborn son to Australia, where I continued my theological studies at Avondale College, that my appreciation of the writings of Ellen White began to change. In Australia I saw and experienced what God can do for His church if we faithfully follow the counsels He has given to us through the gift of prophecy. The many schools, hospitals, and health-food factories and the vibrancy of the churches in that division in the 1960s convinced me that indeed God's counsel through His servant Ellen G. White is invaluable.

Since graduating from Avondale College in 1970, my life and my ministry have been tremendously enriched by the writings of Ellen White. For my personal devotions, I have made it a practice to read and meditate on a portion of Scripture and read two pages from one of Mrs. White's books, and for family worship we always read one of her books either for morning or evening worship. In this way, I have read most of her published works, some books more than once. In my ministry on three continents (Europe, North America, and Australia) and in my travels throughout the world in my work for the Biblical Research Institute of the General Conference, I have witnessed that the work is growing in those fields where the writings of Ellen White are respected and listened to, while it languishes in fields where her writings are neglected.

I close this study with an appeal Elder Denton Rebok made to our church:

> Brethren and sisters of the Advent family, let us . . . take our stand with the remnant church for the message given to us as a people, and for the messenger whom God chose to accomplish His will and purpose in and for us as probationary time comes to an end, as history comes to its last chapter, as Christ finishes His work for the salvation of men, and as closing events in the great controversy bring us ever nearer to the grand consummation of all things earthly.[5]

Endnotes

Chapter 1: Heaven's Means of Communication

1. Peter van Bemmelen, "Revelation and Inspiration," in *Handbook of Seventh-day Adventist Theology,* Raoul Dederen, ed. (Hagerstown, Md.: Review and Herald®, 2000), 28.

2. John Stott, *Romans* (Downers Grove, Ill.: InterVarsity, 1994), 286.

3. Jack J. Blanco, *The Clear Word* (2000).

4. John Murray, *The Epistle to the Romans,* New International Commentary on the New Testament (Grand Rapids, Mich.: Wm. B. Eerdmans, 1965), 73.

5. "The church is God's appointed agency for the salvation of men." Ellen G. White, *The Acts of the Apostles* (Mountain View, Calif.: Pacific Press®, 1911), 9. See also SC 81; YRP 47; RH, July 16, 1895; RH, August 22, 1899; etc.

Chapter 2: The Prophetic Gift

1. H. B. Huffmon, "Prophecy," *Anchor Bible Dictionary,* David Noel Freedman, ed. (New York: Doubleday, 1992), 5:447.

2. Justine Glass, *They Foresaw the Future* (New York: G. P. Putnam's Sons, 1969), 120.

3. Ibid., 155, 224, 228.

4. R. K. Harrison, *Introduction to the Old Testament* (Grand Rapids, Mich.: Wm. B. Eerdmans, 1969), 742.

Endnotes

5. Ibid.

6. Abraham Heschel, *The Prophets* (New York: Harper and Row, 1962), 2:259.

7. J. K. Hoffmeier, "Zipporah," *The International Standard Bible Encyclopedia*, G. W. Bromiley, ed. (Grand Rapids, Mich.: Wm. B. Eerdmans, 1988), 4:1201.

8. Gerhard Friedrich, "*Prophētēs*," *Theological Dictionary of the New Testament*, Gerhard Friedrich, ed., G. W. Bromiley, trans. (Grand Rapids, Mich.: Wm. B. Eerdmans, 1964–74), 6:837.

Chapter 3: Spiritual Gifts and Counterfeits

1. Quoted in James A. Beverley, *Holy Laughter and the Toronto Blessing* (Grand Rapids, Mich.: Zondervan, 1995), 11.

2. Robert Hough, *Toronto Life Magazine*, February 1995, 31; quoted in Beverley, 12.

3. William Welmes, "Letter to the Editor," *Christianity Today*, 8 (Nov. 8, 1963), 19, 20.

4. William J. Samarin, *Tongues of Men and Angels* (New York: Macmillan, 1972), 2.

5. Charles Hunter, "Receiving the Baptism with the Holy Spirit," *Charisma* (July 1989), 54; quoted in John F. Mac Arthur, *Charismatic Chaos* (Grand Rapids, Mich.: Zondervan, 1992), 221.

6. Mac Arthur, 221.

7. W. A. Nolan, *Healing: A Doctor in Search of a Miracle* (New York: Random House, 1974), 259, 260.

8. Beverley, 124.

9. Eric E. Wright, *Strange Fire* (Durham, England: Evangelical Press, 1996), 291.

10. Ibid., 161.

11. Wayne Grudem, "Should Christians Expect Miracles Today?" in G. S. Greig and K. N. Springer, eds., *The Kingdom and the Power* (Ventura, Calif.: Regal Books, 1993), 79.

12. MacArthur, 67.

13. Eoin Giller, e-mail, April 18, 1998.

14. Ibid.

Chapter 4: The Gift of Prophecy and God's Remnant Church

1. M. E. Osterhaven, "Testimony," *The Zondervan Pictorial Encyclopedia of the Bible* (Grand Rapids, Mich.: Zondervan, 1975), 5:682; see also Petros Vassiliades, "The Translation of *Marturia Iesou* in Revelation," *Bible Translator* 36 (1985): 129–34; David E. Aune, *Revelation 1–5*, Word Biblical Commentary (Dallas, Tex.: Word Books, 1997), 80, 81.

2. Ray F. Robbins, *The Revelation of Jesus Christ* (Nashville, Tenn.: Broadman Press, 1975), 154; see also G. R. Beasley-Murray, *The Book of Revelation*, New Century Bible (London: Marshall, Morgan & Scott, 1974), 206.

3. James Moffat, "The Revelation of St. John the Divine," *The Expositor's Greek Testament*, W. R. Nicoll, ed. (Grand Rapids, Mich.: Wm. B. Eerdmans, 1956), 5:465.

4. See G. Pfandl, "The Remnant Church and the Spirit of Prophecy," *Symposium on Revelation—Book II*, Daniel and Revelation Committee Series, F. B. Holbrook, ed. (Silver Spring, Md.: Biblical Research Institute, 1992), 7:305, 306.

5. Hermann Strathmann, "*Martus* ktl.," *Theological Dictionary of the New Testament*, G. Kittel, ed., G. W. Bromiley, trans. (Grand Rapids, Mich.: Wm. B. Eerdmans, 1967), 4:501.

6. Moffat, 5:465.

7. Bernard Grossfeld, *The Targum Onqelos to Genesis*, The Aramaic Bible, Martin McNamara, ed. (Collegeville, Minn.: The Liturgical Press, 1988), 138.

8. Grossfeld, *The Targum Onqelos to Leviticus and Numbers*, The Aramaic Bible, Martin McNamara, ed. (Collegeville, Minn.: The Liturgical Press, 1988), 102, 145. Other occurrences are Exod. 35:31; Num. 11:17, 25, 26, 29; 24:2; Judg. 3:10; 1 Sam. 10:6; 19:10, 23; 2 Sam. 23:2; 1 Kings 22:24; 2 Chron. 15:1; 18:22, 23; 20:14; Ps. 51:13; Isa. 11:2.

9. J. P. Schäfer, "Die Termini 'Heiliger Geist' und 'Geist der Prophetie' in den Targumim und das Verhältnis der Targumim zueinander," *Vetus Testamentum* 20 (1970): 310. The translation is my own.

10. F. F. Bruce, *The Time Is Fulfilled* (Grand Rapids, Mich.: Wm. B. Eerdmans, 1978), 105, 106.

11. Pfandl, 312, 313.

12. G. I. Butler, "Visions and Prophecy," *Review and Herald*, June 2, 1874, 193.

Endnotes

Chapter 5: The Inspiration of the Prophets

1. Henry H. Morris, *Many Infallible Proofs* (San Diego, Calif.: Creation-Life Publishers, 1974), 157.

2. Walter A. Elwell, ed., *Evangelical Dictionary of Theology* (Grand Rapids, Mich.: Baker Book House, 1984), 142.

3. Peter van Bemmelen, "Revelation Inspiration," in *Handbook of Seventh-day Adventist Theology*, Raoul Dederen, ed. (Hagerstown, Md.: Review and Herald®, 2000), 38.

4. George E. Rice, *Luke, a Plagiarist?* (Mountain View, Calif.: Pacific Press®, 1983), 22.

5. GCB 1893, 19, 20.

6. Francis M. Wilcox, *The Testimony of Jesus* (Washington, D.C.: Review and Herald®, 1944), 64.

7. W. C. White Letter to W. W. Eastman, Nov. 4, 1912, (3SM 446).

Chapter 6: Testing the Prophets

1. *Seventh-day Adventist Yearbook 2007* (Silver Spring, Md.: General Conference of Seventh-day Adventists, 2007), 7.

2. A. G. Daniells, *The Abiding Gift of Prophecy* (Mountain View, Calif.: Pacific Press®, 1936), 307.

3. Quoted in *The Spirit of Prophecy Treasure Chest* (Glendale, Calif.: Prophetic Guidance School of the Voice of Prophecy, 1960), 25.

4. *Centennial Book of Modern Spiritualism in America* (Chicago: The National Spiritualist Association of United States of America, 1948), 115, 68.

5. F. M. Wilcox, *The Testimony of Jesus* (Washington, D.C.: Review and Herald®, 1944), 35.

6. Wilcox, "The Testimony of Jesus," *Review and Herald*, June 9, 1946, 61.

Chapter 7: The Work of the Prophets

1. For example, *Review and Herald*, Sept. 12, 1871; Mar. 13, 1894; *Signs of the Times*, Aug. 16, 23, 30, Sept. 6, 13, Nov. 29, Dec. 6, 20, 1877.

2. For example, *Review and Herald*, May 27, July 29, 1902; Feb. 10, 17, 24, Mar. 3, 1910.

3. L. H. Christian, *The Fruitage of Spiritual Gifts* (Washington, D.C.: Review and Herald®, 1947), 218.

4. Arthur L. White, *Ellen G. White: The Early Years* (Hagerstown, Md.: Review and Herald®, 1985), 103.

5. Ibid., 104.

6. See ibid., 490–492.

7. Ibid., 492.

8. Keith A. Fournier and W. D. Watkins, *A House United?* (Colorado Springs, Colo.: Navpress, 1994), 337.

9. Charles Colson and Richard J. Neuhaus, eds., *Evangelicals and Catholics Together: Toward a Common Mission* (Dallas: Word Publishing, 1995), 108.

Chapter 8: The Authority of the Prophets

1. General Conference of Seventh-day Adventists, "The Inspiration and Authority of the Ellen G. White Writings," *Ministry* 55, no. 8 (August 1982): 21.

2. Ibid.

3. J. J. Robertson, *The White Truth* (Mountain View, Calif.: Pacific Press®, 1981), 60.

4. Roger L. Dudley and Des Cummings Jr., "Who Reads Ellen White?" *Ministry* 55, no. 10 (October 1982): 10.

5. James White, in *A Word to the "Little Flock"* (Brunswick, Maine: James White, 1847), 13.

6. *Review and Herald*, Dec. 4, 1855, 79.

7. *Review and Herald*, Feb. 14, 1871, 68.

8. "Fundamental Beliefs," *Seventh-day Adventist Yearbook 2007* (Silver Spring, Md.: General Conference of Seventh-day Adventists, 2007), 7.

Chapter 9: The Integrity of the Prophetic Gift

1. Merlin D. Burt, "Ellen White and the Shut Door," *"Ellen White and Current Issues" Symposium*, Center for Adventist Research, vol. 1 (2005): 73.

2. E. G. White in *A Word to the "Little Flock"* (Brunswick, Maine: James White, 1847), 14.

3. Ibid.

4. Ellen G. Harmon, "Letter from Sister Harmon," *Day Star*, March 14, 1846, 7 (written Feb. 15, 1846).

5. *A Word to the "Little Flock,"* 19.

6. Herbert E. Douglass, *Messenger of the Lord* (Nampa, Idaho: Pacific Press®, 1998), 552.

7. The interview was published in the *Los Angeles Times* dated October 23, 1980.

8. "There Simply Is No Case," *Review and Herald,* Sept. 17, 1981, 3, 5.

9. George H. Callcott, *History in the United States, 1800–1860: Its Practice and Purpose* (Baltimore, Md.: The Johns Hopkins Press, 1970), 128, 129.

10. Ibid., 134.

11. Ibid., 136.

12. W. C. White, "Brief Statements Regarding the Writings of Ellen G. White," reprint (St. Helena, Calif.: Elmshaven Office of the Ellen G. White Estate, 1933), 5.

13. See the introduction to *The Great Controversy,* xii.

14. Douglass, 468.

15. *The Independent,* Aug. 23, 1915; quoted in A. L. White, *Ellen G. White: Messenger to the Remnant,* 126.

Chapter 10: The End-time Prophet and End-time Events

1. L. P. Tolhurst, "The Death Decree in the Setting of the Final Crisis," unpublished manuscript, 2.

Chapter 11: Interpreting the Prophetic Writings

1. Raoul Dederen, "Ellen White's Doctrine of Scripture," in "Are There Prophets in the Modern Church?" Supplement to *Ministry* (July 1977): 24H.

2. Arthur L. White, *Ellen G. White: The Early Elmshaven Years, 1900–1905* (Washington, D.C.: Review and Herald®, 1981), 72.

3. W. C. White Letter to S. N. Haskell, October 31, 1912.

4. Ibid.

Chapter 12: The Blessings of the Prophetic Gift

1. This story was adapted from J. N. Loughborough, *The Great Second Advent Movement* (Nashville, Tenn.: Southern Publishing Association, 1905), 230–232.

2. *Review and Herald,* Feb. 3, 1859, 87.

3. Emmett K. Vande Vere, *The Wisdom Seekers* (Nashville, Tenn.: Southern Publishing Association, 1972), 59.

4. Don F. Neufeld, ed., *Seventh-day Adventist Encyclopedia* (Washington, D.C.: Review and Herald®, 1976), 47.

5. D. E. Robinson, *The Story of Our Health Message*, 3rd enlarged ed. (Nashville, Tenn.: Southern Publishing Association, 1965), 66.

6. Ibid., 67.

7. Leonard Brand and Don S. McMahon, *The Prophet and Her Critics* (Nampa, Idaho: Pacific Press®, 2005), 77, 78.

8. Ibid., 51.

9. Ibid., 73.

10. A. G. Daniells, *The Abiding Gift of Prophecy* (Mountain View, Calif.: Pacific Press®, 1936), 336, 337.

11. Arthur L. White, *Ellen G. White: The Early Elmshaven Years, 1900–1905* (Washington, D.C.: Review and Herald®, 1981), 297, 298.

12. Ibid., 298.

13. Daniells, 340.

Chapter 13: Confidence in the Prophetic Gift

1. Adapted from *Scope*, Summer 2005, 6, 7.

2. J. N. Loughborough, *The Great Second Advent Movement* (Nashville, Tenn.: Southern Publishing Association, 1905), 182.

3. Adapted from Denton E. Rebok, *Believe His Prophets* (Washington, D.C.: Review and Herald®, 1958), 309–312.

4. J. N. Andrews, *Review and Herald*, February 15, 1870, 65.

5. Rebok, 320.